Sicilian
Food & Wine
The Cognoscente's Guide

Francesca Lombardo
Jacqueline Alio

Trinacria Editions
New York

Published by Trinacria Editions, New York.

Legal Deposit: Library of Congress, British Library (and Bodleian Libraries, Cambridge University Library, Trinity College Library), Italian National Libraries (Rome, Florence, Palermo).

Illustrations, photography, maps and cover design by Louis Mendola.

Printed in the United States of America on acid-free paper.

10 9 8 7 6 5 4 3 2

ISBN 9780991588633 (print)
ISBN 9781943639991 (ebook)

Library of Congress Control Number 2014952285

A CIP catalogue record for this book is available from the British Library.

IN MEMORIAM

Anna Vitale
Grazia Alio

ABOUT THE AUTHORS

Francesca Lombardo and Jacqueline Alio are connoisseurs, gastronomes, cooks and scholars. A book about Sicilian cuisine written in English by Sicilians in Sicily is the rarest of rarities. There is no substitute for living in Sicily through several annual culinary seasons, year after year, understanding the Sicilian language and experiencing the island's complex culture, the essence of what makes it unique. It is equally important to understand the salient role played by Sicilian food, wine and agriculture in the wider context of the Mediterranean, Europe and indeed the world. Over the last decade, the authors' online articles have been read by millions.

Francesca Lombardo is a recognized wine expert certified by the Italian Sommeliers Association. Fluent in four languages, she is a high school teacher, culinary travel consultant and food writer.

Jacqueline Alio wrote *Women of Sicily: Saints, Queens and Rebels.* A historian of note, she co-authored *The Peoples of Sicily: A Multicultural Legacy,* an ethnographic history of medieval Sicily.

PROLOGUE
Palermo 1994

Nearly two hundred Sicilians are gathered at a stately home surrounded by gardens on the edge of a chaotic city. The Winter evening is breezy and cool — the temperature that of earliest Autumn in London or New York — but devoid of rain. A few of the guests are chatting beneath the stars on the large terrace, where they can smoke without censure. Inside, the guests sip cocktails in a large Baroque salon. The men are wearing dark suits, while many of the women are dressed in black, some in evening gowns, yet the atmosphere is anything but somber. By eight o'clock most of the guests have arrived.

Some of the attendees seem to know each other, but a few foreign faces are seeded among the cosmopolitan crowd, and many of the gentlemen introduce themselves by colorful phrases redolent of another age: Lanza di Trabia, Paternò di Spedolotto, Moncada di Monforte. Anachronistically, their surnames are followed by the multisyllabic names of the dukedoms and baronies that belonged to their feudal ancestors, for this evening shall be remembered, decades later, as the last great gathering of the local aristocracy to be seen in western Sicily.

If the occasion is arcane it is very real. Sicily's royal family, the dynasty that reigned until 1861, has come to commemorate one of their own, Francesco de Bourbon, a king who died in exile in 1894. The monarch whose favorite food earned him the nickname "The Lasagna King."

Their host is Count Giuseppe Tasca d'Almerita, Sicily's premier vintner and a pioneering Sicilian oenologist, who usually resides among the vast vineyards of Regaleali, his estate in the Sicanian Mountains, but this evening stands by the door with his graceful wife to greet every guest that arrives. His children and grandchildren help out, just as they do at the winery. Count Tasca's role transcends that of host, for he is the Sicilian representative of the royal family, their delegate in what used to be the Kingdom of Sicily. According to traditional protocol, the Bourbons arrive last.

As one might expect, the wine served here at Villa Tasca is the Count's, but the invitation to this *serata* didn't mention much more than the Bourbons' attendance. Prince Ferdinando — also a vintner — lives with his wife in the South of France, while his cousin Prince Giuseppe lives in Madrid, where he writes about cuisine for Condé Nast. Princess Urraca, another cousin, lives in Munich. Prince Carlo, Ferdinando's son and heir, is also here this evening.

At half past eight, food begins to appear on a series of large tables at the center of the grand ballroom, brought out not by waiters but by liveried footmen. What, ponders an American present, might be served at this most uncommon event?

Anybody expecting the parsimonious offerings served at diplomatic receptions around Europe is about to be pleasantly surprised, and delightfully overwhelmed. What arrives is a multi-course dinner beginning with — Sicilian street food!

The first thing that one can identify are huge silver platters piled high, pyramid style, with golden *arancini,* saffron rice balls stuffed with beef or ham. Each crusty *arancina* is the size of a tennis ball, a meal in itself. (An *arancina* is shown on this book's front cover.)

Beside these, the footmen arrange nine or ten slightly smaller platters layered with *panelle,* flat chickpea fritters. Next to those there are Sicilian croquettes, made with potatoes, cheese and mint. There are even slender cardoon stalks fried in a thick batter. And artichoke hearts.

On the other side of the table, flanked by towering stacks of white china plates bearing the same Tasca coat of arms that graces the labels on Regaleali's wine bottles, appear two gigantic platters of *caponata,* Sicilian aubergine salad.

Complementing these appetizers, another table bears the weight of the main courses: octopus salad, meatballs in a white sauce, stuffed swordfish rolls, tiny scrolls of Nebrodian ham.

There seem to be *mountains* of food. There are bowls of roasted Sicilian chestnuts, and half a dozen types of olive, the latter ranging in color from pale green to gray to black. Even a few plates of the stuffed herring Sicilians call *beccafico.*

The wine keeps flowing. Mostly white and mostly chilled. Enough of it to feed a small lake. The Sicilian guests are happy. The foreign ones are astounded by the lavishness of this "informal" dinner attended by royalty.

Another hour passes and dessert arrives, a little after ten. *Cannoli* and *cassata* are the stars here. Tiny glasses of *limoncello* and *passito* are offered. And espresso.

It has been an evening fit for a would-be king.

PREFACE

"Cù si marita, sta cuntenti un giornu, cù ammazza nu porcu, sta cuntenti un'annu."

— Sicilian Proverb

"One who gets married will be happy for a day," says the old proverb, "but one who butchers a pig will be happy for a year."

Food is about more than eating. Cuisine is a reflection of a community's soul. Sharing it, "breaking bread" together, can traverse the chasms that sometimes divide us.

Dining has been a communal activity since the days when our neolithic forebears hunted together. Indeed, Sicily was one of the first parts of Europe to benefit from the introduction of agriculture, some ten millennia ago. So venerable is Sicily's culinary history that, inevitably, the island is inextricably linked to certain foods. The Siceliot city of Selinus took its name from *selinon,* the wild celery that grew there. The associations of certain fruits — like Persephone's Sicilian pomegranate — are almost mystical. In Sicily we find the manna ash and the citron, the Hebrews' *etrog,* both replete with Biblical significance. Wine, of course, has given birth to an entire culture. It was probably the Greeks who brought domesticated grapes to southern Italy, and the Romans who planted the first domesticated cultivars in France.

Among Sicily's anomalies is the world's oldest chestnut tree, miraculously preserved on the slopes of Mount Etna. This region is where ice cream is thought to have been invented, with runners bringing snow to the luxurious Roman villas below.

More than the localized cuisines of most regions, Sicily's mirrors a truly multicultural past, bringing the world of the medieval Normans and Swabians to the wider environment of Fatimids, Jews and Byzantine Greeks, forming a culinary bridge from Europe to Africa to Asia via the Mediterranean.

This book is a guide to a distinctive cuisine. Unlike most publications that focus on cookery, it is not a cookbook, although a few of the simplest, classic Sicilian recipes are included, particularly two or three overlooked by most authors.

These pages are intended to be an anchor, a ready reference to consult before taking your first steps into the eclectic world of Sicilian food and wine. This book is not meant to take the place of the numerous Sicilian cookbooks and recipe websites, but to complement them, and you need not be an aficionado or even a very competent cook to appreciate the information presented in the following pages.

Before sampling food and seeking recipes, you must know what is on offer. This book is the roadmap that will make you a full-fledged *cognoscente*.

It is impossible to cover every single culinary detail of the last three millennia, and recipes themselves vary by locality, family and each chef's interpretation. The canon, such as it is, is fluid, even idiosyncratic, and this guide should not be construed as dogma. Nobody can know everything about Sicilian cuisine and Sicily's myriad variations on each traditional recipe.

Yes, this is a guide to *traditional* Sicilian cuisine. While it may serve as a springboard for chefs creating new renditions of classic recipes, it represents what gradually evolved in Sicily over the course of centuries, not what is being "reinvented" today in restaurants in Italy and around the world. Profiles of such foods as "Sicilian sushi" lie beyond the scope of this monograph.

Most Italian *cognoscenti* agree that the flavors grow more intense, perhaps more satisfying, as you make your way down the peninsula toward Sicily, and we are inclined to agree. It was an observation made by Elizabeth Gilbert, author of *Eat, Pray, Love,* whose travels took her to Sicily. In her memoir, food was an integral part of a spiritual journey, perhaps the most facile facet of a personal catharsis.

In learning about food, let's not forget to enjoy it.

Buon appetito!

CONTENTS

INTRODUCTION

"For there you may admire vines revelling both in the richness of their fertile clumps and the excellence of their remarkable tendrils. There you can see orchards that evoke praise for the astonishing variety of their fruits."

— Hugh Falcandus, *Letter to Peter, Treasurer of Palermo*

Most of us eat what we enjoy, apart, perhaps, from the occasional dietary restriction due to voluntary philosophical proscriptions or pragmatic health concerns. While we may be inclined, at least occasionally, to think about the nutritional value of the foods we consume, we are less likely to contemplate the cultural relevance of the wine we sip or the historic origin of the spaghetti we so joyfully entwine between the prongs of a fork.

In 1958, Gore Vidal found himself working as a last-minute script editor on *Ben Hur* in Rome's Cinecittà. Wanting to add a splash of color to a bowl of fruit and vegetables in a scene about to be filmed, he was surprised when both of his suggestions — a red pepper and crimson tomatoes — were flatly turned down. Vidal was politely but firmly reminded that both species were indigenous to the Americas, and thus unknown to the ancient Romans.

You can savor a certain dish without knowing its ingredients, its provenance, its history or how it was prepared. No, you need not know the traditions associated with food to enjoy it. In our global village, much of what we consume traverses ethnicities, continents and oceans to please our eager palates.

For the most part, that is a good thing. Localized production means that fresh sushi, to cite but a single popular example, is available far beyond Japan's shores. Some foods are ennobled by distance. Arugula, which began its life in Italy as an unpretentious weed, has become something special in Britain and in the United States.

But for those who aspire to learn something about a culture, to experience its nuances, there's no substitute for knowing at least a little about its cuisine. Knowing that Pliny the Elder described Sicilian capers may not alter their taste or form, but it provides the green buds with an identity beyond their tart flavor. American president Thomas Jefferson's appreciation of Marsala, which he served in the White House, is a reminder that certain tastes are nearly universal.

In our minds, certain foods have become inseparable from the peoples who popularized them, part of a cultural identity. It is partly for this reason that Italians object to foreigners' generic use of the demonym *Parmesan,* which in Italy refers exclusively to Parmigiano Reggiano cheese. Of course, those who advertise food products would prefer that we recognized in certain brands something beyond mere taste.

From its Alpine North to its Mediterranean South, Italy boasts a greater diversity of indigenous flora than any other European country except Russia. This has spawned a great variety of edible plants and hence foods. In Sicily, the diversity grew with each successive invasion, leaving us with a rather wide choice for a region comparable in size to Albania, Wales or Massachusetts.

A few Sicilian foods have wended their way into the public mind beyond Italy. Here the *cannolo* comes to mind.

For the most part, the topics in this volume speak for themselves. As we have mentioned, our emphasis is the traditional, the historical, the classic, the timeless, not the whimsical *nouvelle cuisine* invented the day before yesterday only to disappear the day after tomorrow. In our opinion, too many of today's Sicilian chefs, in aspiring to rock-star status, formulate trendy or "creative" recipes too eccentric for most diners' tastes, dishes that find embodiment in a few morsels of food served on an enormous white plate, usually at an equally inordinate price. Even some vintners have fallen prey to this mentality, striving to become "personalities," as if each were a budding Picasso.

As we explained at the beginning, this is not a recipe book. Among the handful of traditional recipes presented here are two or three that we have never seen published anyplace else; those for Sicilian poultry stuffing and Sicilian eggnog stand out in this regard. Excluded from consideration were recipes for which the ingredients might not be found very easily outside Italy. To that end, we spent time during our frequent travels in Britain, Canada and the United States confirming the availability of certain products.

There are, of course, a number of recipe collections dedicated to Sicilian cuisine. Nowadays, somebody searching for a particular recipe need venture no further than the internet, where several variations of each are likely to be revealed. Here the reader is reminded that there are very few "canonical" recipes for most traditional Sicilian specialties, many of which vary slightly by locality, either in their ingredients or in their preparation.

We were the first writers to break the news, back in 2009 (on a popular website), that ancient Kalamata olive cultivars survive in Sicily. This we did without mentioning a location except, with deliberate inexactitude, "western Sicily." Although we remain sworn to secrecy, we can reveal that the exemplar tested genetically still thrives in an olive grove in the Hyblaean Mountains southwest of Siracusa (anciently Syracuse), and we have indicated its location on our map of olive varieties.

Throughout this book, we have striven for accuracy without pedantry. We'll be fair, explaining that *arugula* is what most

Britons call *rocket salad,* and that their *aubergines* are the Americans' *eggplants.* And that *sparacelli* is either wild asparagus or semi-domesticated broccoli, depending on where you are in Sicily.

The glossary mentions a few terms not covered at length in the chapters. Many entries found there are simple translations. The objective was to list those Sicilian terms most likely to be encountered, excluding the more arcane or localized ones. You may find that some of our translations differ from those of other authors writing in English.

An effort has been made to include in the following pages the foods that make Sicilian cuisine uniquely Sicilian. Unlike the overwhelming majority of books dedicated to Sicilian cuisine — or, for that matter, Sicilian history — this one does not identify Sicily or its unique culinary heritage merely as "regional" fractions of a greater Italian whole. Without overlooking Italy, our island and its culture are viewed from a more cosmopolitan perspective. Sicilian culinary history traces its eclectic origins from antiquity, when Sicily was part of *Magna Graecia,* more than two millennia before there emerged a nation state known as *Italy* (in 1861). Under the Arabs Sicily was a Fatimid emirate, and the Normans made it a European kingdom.

Speaking of terminology, a few points should be made regarding context and the presentation of details. In other words, the most accurate information possible. A few historical Sources we have consulted are mentioned in a section preceding our Acknowledgments.

What you shall read here, especially where history and culture are concerned, may vary a bit from the observations of other food and wine authors who, we believe, have sometimes extrapolated beyond what reality suggests, something we are extremely reluctant to do. When it comes to history, recipes and traditions, any food writer worth her salt should check and recheck her sources, and perhaps her powers of observation.

To avoid misleading you, we have not generalized details, anecdotes, or personal experiences into "facts" about a population of millions.

It's about the food. This guide really isn't the place for a personal "statement." To us, the most important message of food is that it brings people together.

Another issue begs to be addressed, *per forza*.

Considering objectivity paramount, we were, and remain, extremely reluctant to shill for this or that winery or eatery. Here the lone exceptions are Giuseppe Tasca d'Almerita (1913-1998), who played a singular role at the vanguard of estate wine production during the 1960s, and the Alliata family before him.

In general, however, we prefer not to mention individuals or firms unless it is genuinely necessary, and we are beholden to none.

There is a very pragmatic reasoning behind our policy. The food and wine authors who fill their books with much information about restaurants and wineries run the very real risk of their writings becoming dated as those firms go out of business. That is a fact of life here in Sicily. It is our opinion that the internet obviates the need for such a practice, and anyway there are travel guides, with their frequent updates, to assist travelers.

In writing this book, we have endeavored to provide you with something accessible and enduring, seeking to emphasize the practical over the esoteric.

Various food and wine critics have noted the prevalence of bias and cronyism in a field full of gifts, perks and promotions, something we have sought to avoid. Fruit of a fully independent effort, this book is what the trade used to call "free press." The publisher and authors have received no gifts, sponsorship or financing of any kind, either directly or indirectly, from restaurateurs, vintners, public agencies, travel bureaux or professional trade associations, nor do they own a restaurant or winery. They do not market food products or wines.

Our objectivity is, we hope, beyond cavil.

Most books about Sicilian food are, literally and figuratively, more colorful than this one. While we hope that you'll find this book useful, it is the kind of reference one consults for reliable information rather than fanciful narrative and attractive pictures. Here we were inspired by the classic culinary guides and recipe books published before the twentieth century.

This book is imbued with our passion but not with information about our intimate lives, and in that respect it differs slightly from a few of the more popular, trendier Sicilian cookbooks and wine guides currently in print in English. Much as we love culinary literature, this is not a "culinary memoir." We are not "innocents abroad," and we'll avoid *protagonismo* (making ourselves the focus). Sicily is ours, and we shall try to make it *yours* too. Here you will not read the kind of introspective commentary that views Sicily as an untamed, foreign place, or the setting of its author's existential crisis. Sicily has never been "foreign" to us, and we know who we are.

For its amalgamation of cultures, Sicily has been called The World's Island. Through these pages, two "native daughters" hope to bring some of the pleasures of our magical island into your life. In the process, you may become a true *Siculophile,* a lover of Sicily and its culture.

MAPS

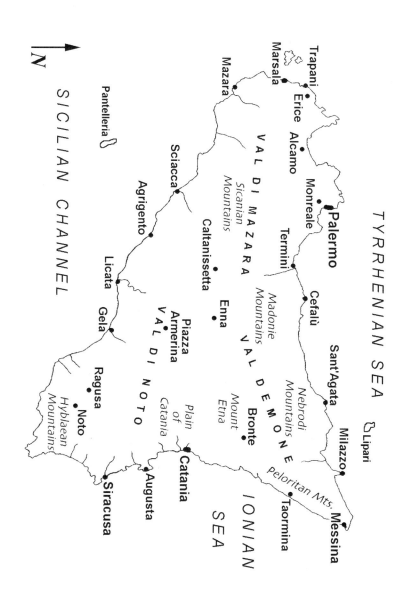

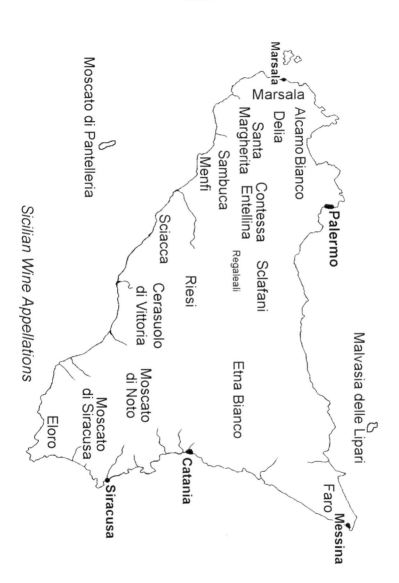

Sicilian Wine Appellations

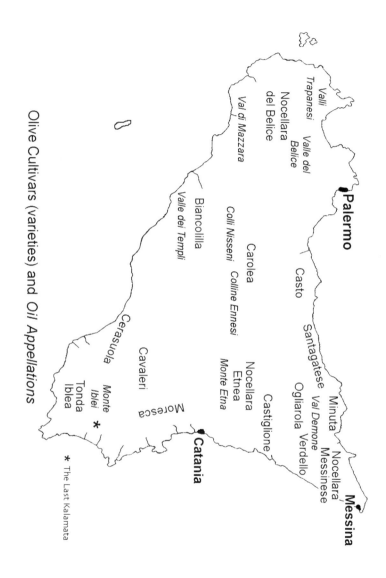

Olive Cultivars (varieties) and *Oil Appellations*

* The Last Kalamata

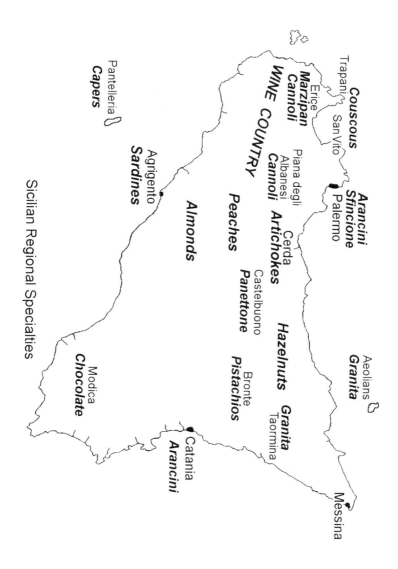

Sicilian Regional Specialties

Pantelleria
Capers

Trapani
Couscous

Erice
Marzipan
Cannoli
WINE COUNTRY

San Vito

Arancini
Sfincione
Palermo

Piana degli
Albanesi
Cannoli

Cerda
Artichokes

Agrigento
Sardines

Almonds

Peaches

Castelbuono
Panettone

Hazelnuts

Bronte
Pistachios

Aeolians
Granita

Granita
Taormina

Modica
Chocolate

Catania
Arancini

Messina

Stencil for the paper wrapping of Sicilian lemons sold in Great Britain by the firm founded by the author's grandfather in 1926

CHAPTER 1

The Art of Sicilian Dining

"Then you would not approve of Syracusan dinners, and the refinements of Sicilian cookery?"

— Plato, *The Republic*

To the uninitiated, the art of Sicilian dining is elusive, an object of mystery, something vaguely perceived but not yet experienced. Something complex, only partly "Italian." Every place has its own style of eating to complement its style of cooking. Sicily's owes much to her Arab and Baroque traditions, colored by some religious customs and perhaps even a few habits known in Plato's time. It is, in its own way, conventional, but not especially ritualistic.

One must question whether any other place in Europe has brought dining to the level, if not the exalted status, of high art the way Sicily has. It's not the number of courses in the typical meal that makes the Sicilian approach distinctive, but the way each dish is served, really a meeting of the ways between the best folk traditions and the best aristocratic ones. And, of course, a *fusion* — to use a fashionable term sometimes applied to Sicilian cuisine — that bridges three Mediterranean continents.

There is no "typical" Sicilian meal, but there is a well-established approach, and here we should perhaps start at the beginning.

Aperitifs are often offered but rarely obligatory. The *antipasti* (appetizers or starters) are usually more filling than what you would have elsewhere: *arancini,* potato croquettes, squares of *sfincione* (a Sicilian pizza without cheese), ceci fritters, *caponata,* salamis, cheeses. The Sicilian term *stuzzichini* hardly does justice to this assortment of delights, some of which have "transitioned" their way into the realm of "street food."

Then there's the *primo,* usually a pasta or rice dish, or perhaps a soup or couscous. This is followed by the *secondo,* the main course, perhaps accompanied by a *contorno* (side-dish) and served with mineral water and wine. By tradition, main courses are meat or fish.

After this there's fruit followed by coffee, dessert and a liqueur or sweet dessert wine. Of course, if you wish you can content yourself with just some pasta or a salad. In the case of a complete meal, it's difficult to imagine enjoying all of this in less than an hour. Or wanting to.

Though one occasionally laments long lunches that break the weekday in two (afternoon shop and office closings from one to four are still known in Sicily), there's something to be said for indulging in great food made from the freshest ingredients.

Sicilian cuisine is an ensemble of strong, distinctive flavors, whether it's local lamb, fresh tuna (nothing like the canned variety) or swordfish steaks, sea urchins, aged cheeses made from goat's or sheep's milk, or the island's unique wines — Nero d'Avola is one of the world's heartiest reds, and the whites are far from bland.

Here we encounter some geographic differences that are logical but often overlooked — the varying cuisines of mountain communities compared to those of seaside towns, and the invisible line running between Enna and Caltanissetta that divides the island into east and west.

In Sicily, nothing is ever meant to be subtle to the point of being ignored, and no sauce or condiment ever overshadows the main show. Even the ice creams seem to have more flavor than their European and American counterparts.

There's nothing excessively formal or ritualistic here; pasta to Italians enjoys none of the mystical esteem accorded rice by the Japanese. Sicilians might worship at the altar of good food, but they prefer eating what they find there.

Yet the seeming chaos created by a latitude in choices doesn't mean that Sicilian cuisine lacks for social conventions. Coffees, such as *cappuccino,* containing milk are rarely consumed after noon, and — in a place where alcoholism is virtually unknown — it's not at all unusual for young teenagers to enjoy a glass of wine or *limoncello,* a sweet lemon liqueur.

Colazione, breakfast, was traditionally more substantial than the "continental" breakfast of coffee and a *cornetto* that became popular during the twentieth century as Italy's population gradually became more urban. It might be a large cup of coffee consisting mostly of milk, along with a piece of cheese and seasonal fruit or a *frittata,* an omelet — the classic country meal.

Served around one in the afternoon, lunch, now called *pranzo,* is a more substantial meal. Until recent times, it was the day's principal meal, but for most families that is now the case only on Sundays.

The evening meal, nowadays called *cena*, is served around eight in the evening, and that is the hour when most pizzerias and other restaurants open.

Here a few simple definitions are in order.

Ristorante - a rather formal restaurant; expect uniformed waiters or waitresses and a good but pricey menu.

Trattoria - a less formal restaurant, though a *trattoria* meal can cost as much as one in a *ristorante*. Some "trattorias" in Palermo and Catania are quite pricey. (Any Sicilian who calls his trendy *trattoria* a *bistro* should be sent back to cooking school.)

Osteria - a small restaurant, in theory less formal than a *trattoria* and less expensive, offering a limited menu. However, like *trattoria,* the word *osteria* has been hijacked by the greedy owners of a few pricey restaurants in Sicily's largest cities.

Pizzeria - a restaurant specialized in a wide selection of pizzas; typically open only in evenings, some pizzerias serve other simple fare, like pasta.

Polleria - a stand or small shop that serves chicken on a skewer, usually as a take-away food.

Rosticceria - a stand that sells arancine (rice balls) and other fried "street food."

Gelateria - an ice cream parlor or stand, which may also serve various drinks.

Pasticceria - a pastry shop, which may also serve ice cream.

Bar - generic term for a coffee bar which might also serve liquor.

Pub - a British-style pub (more or less), which Americans sometimes call a "club" or "bar."

Drinkeria - a quasi-English word for a pub.

Locale - pub or restaurant generically.

And a few terms describing dining environments:

Cortile - a "courtyard," but the word is used very loosely in Sicily.

Giardino - a garden, though the word is not always used very precisely.

Baglio - an enclosed courtyard in a historic, fortified building resembling a small castle.

Terrazza - usually a rooftop terrace with a view.

A few words about details might be helpful. The *coperto,* which might run to two euros per diner, is a "cover charge" rather than an actual tip. In the days of yore it defrayed the cost of the table cloth and the bread served with most meals, which is why you sometimes encounter the phrase *pane e coperto.* The *coperto* survives because Italian customers are infamously parsimonious tippers, and this is the only way to squeeze a pseudo-gratuity out of them. Incidentally, the standard tip for a meal in a Sicilian restaurant is ten percent, and note that the taxes are included in the final bill. You may console yourself by considering that some restaurants in New York "recommend" a tip of twenty-two percent.

Home-cooked meals, of course, will spare you the need to be familiar with such complexities, and so will street food.

As we shall see, many foods are closely associated with certain feasts and holidays, and some are more generally seasonal. *Gelo di melone,* watermelon gelatin, is a Summer dessert, while marzipan pastry (shown on this book's back cover), makes its appearance in the Autumn. It's a question of harvests, climate and geography as much as tradition.

Let's cast a glance over Sicily's agriculture and culinary history.

CHAPTER 2

The Place and the Cuisine

"The climate's delicate, the air most sweet; Fertile the isle, the temple much surpassing the common praise it bears."

— William Shakespeare, *The Winter Tale*

Food comes to us from the land and the sea. Sicily has plenty of both. Our island was once a patchwork of Greek and Punic colonies. Then it became a Roman province, later an emirate and then a kingdom. Only since 1861 has it been part of a united Italy, and in these pages the word *Italian* will be used sparingly, and mostly as a geographic term rather than a political one. Let's look at Sicily's geography, natural features, agriculture and cuisine, past and present.

The Land

At 25,711 square kilometers (9,927 square miles), Sicily is the largest island in the Mediterranean and the largest of Italy's twenty political regions, slightly larger than Piedmont. For comparison, Wales covers 20,780 square kilometers and Massachusetts 27,340. In addition to the island of Sicily, the region includes a number of coastal and volcanic islands. For centuries Malta and Gozo were part of the Kingdom of Sicily.

The highest peak is Mount Etna, western Europe's largest active volcano, at a variable 3,329 meters (10,922 feet) above sea level, followed by rocky Pizzo Carbonara (at 1,979 meters) and several other summits in the Madonie range, and forested Mount Soro, in the Nebrodi range, at 1,847 meters. All of these peaks are covered with snow for at least two months of the year, Etna usually for three or four.

The longest river is the Salso at 144 kilometers (89 miles), rising in the Madonie Mountains and flowing southward past Enna to Licata, marking Sicily's drainage divide, or watershed. A tributary of the Simeto in western Sicily coincidentally shares the same name. To supply drinking water, there are numerous man-made lakes fed by streams and springs, but Sicily boasts very few natural ones, notably salty Pergusa near Enna and a few in the Nebrodi and Etna regions. None of Sicily's rivers are navigable today. After the Salso the chief rivers – now little more than streams – are the Simeto (114 km), the Belice (107 km), the Dittaino (105 km) and the Platani (103 km). Several are of historical interest. The Platani (the Greeks' Halycos) delineated the boundary between Greeks and Carthaginians according to a treaty of 306 BC (BCE). The Simeto and the Dittaino mark the route of the Normans to the Arab city of Kasr'Janni (Enna) in 1061.

For the most part, the Sicilian landscape we see today bears only the slightest resemblance to what it was like from antiquity into the Middle Ages, no less the seventeenth century. It's not just the urban sprawl that has marred the scenery around Palermo and Catania, but the scars of a long process of overzealous deforestation and mediocre land management across the island.

The idyllic terrain of the island beloved by Phoenicians, Greeks and Romans was full of forests. In most areas they were far more expansive than they are today. Yes, Sicily's wooded mountains are still spectacular. There's Etna, which segues into the Nebrodi and Peloritans, and the Madonie to the west are not to be overlooked. There are isolated but precious jewels like the Ficuzza and Cammarata forest reserves in the Sicanian Mountains.

But by the seventeenth century the fate of the forests around Enna, Agrigento and Caltanissetta was sealed by the need for wheat to feed a growing population and the lust for wood to build ships for an expanding Spanish Empire. Then came the mining for sulphur, marble and limestone.

Most of the rivers were attenuated to streams and, finally, the seasonal "torrents" (run-offs) we have today — some of which being little more than dry creek beds for five or six months of the year. Topographical references written as recently as 1850 mention the fish that flourished in these streams until that era.

The extensive coastline ranges from rocky cliffs to sandy beaches, and the island also offers fascinating natural features like Alcantara Gorge, fed by Etna's snows, caverns like Carburangeli and the gray mud flows formed by sporadic geysers that give Maccalube, near Aragona, its moonlike appearance.

Sicily's chief mountain ranges are distinguished in their limestone formation and, perhaps more obviously, in their vegetation. The stunning Nebrodi Mountains of northeastern Sicily seem to have endured the ages better than the other ranges. The rocky buttes capped by Sutera's monastery and the castles at Mussomeli and Caccamo resemble those that house the Metéora monasteries near Kalambaka in Greece.

In the southeastern corner of the island the Hyblaean Mountains are less imposing, rising gently above graceful slopes. Yet Cavagrande Cassibile, a scenic canyon, was formed here, and the necropoli of Pantalica were fashioned into limestone cliffs in antiquity. The wine country is a hilly region in the west, with Marsala its unofficial capital. Here wheat was cultivated until around 1800.

In addition to its larger protected areas, Sicily has a number of smaller reserves, some of which welcome human visitors. In the southeast the Vendicari Reserve lies along the Ionian coast. In the northwest the Zingaro is the most "people friendly" of the coastal reserves. Near Siracusa there's a reserve at the mouth of the Cyane River where papyrus still grows, and the Biviere di Gela, as well as similar reserves at the mouths of the Simeto and Platani rivers, are stops for migratory birds making their way between Africa and Europe.

Flora and Fauna

Much of the wild vegetation, like the papyrus, palm trees and stone pines, is typically Mediterranean, but certain conifers, including the endangered Nebrodi Fir, are similar to species found in much cooler climates. In the Middle Ages Sicily was significantly cooler than it is today. Global warming explains part of this; rampant deforestation and the gradual decline in precipitation explains the rest. Except for some unusually wet Winters every few years, Sicily's precipitation and temperatures follow a consistent pattern year after year, especially during the torrid Summer. This makes the grape harvests remarkably constant from one season to the next.

Most of Sicily's fauna is hidden from view most of the time. There are more foxes than wolves; the latter are almost all gone. There are few hare, but rabbits abound.

A few wild cats roam the large national park on the slopes of Mount Etna and also the remote parts of the Nebrodi and Madonie; these regal hunters are similar to the striped wild cats found in the Pyrenees. The cats survive because they live in wooded areas on rugged slopes where few humans venture, but they are threatened by hybridization through crossbreeding with the ubiquitous domestic felines.

One still sees the rare beaver or squirrel (one variety of the latter is strikingly similar to the North American chipmunk) in the woods of the Madonie or Nebrodi. The wild boar that has been re-introduced into Sicily is actually a Sardinian variety, though the "domesticated" Nebrodian black swine is perhaps more boar than pig. The local deer, for which the Nebrodi were named by the Greeks (from *nebros* for fawn), were hunted to extinction long ago.

A local species of toad whose body grows to a length of almost 20 centimeters (8 inches) sometimes comes out into the rains, several varieties of frog inhabit the streams, and several varieties of gecko lizard can be seen during warm months. Hermann's tortoise also thrives in Sicily. The nocturnal hedgehog still lives here, though it is only rarely seen. The freshwater fish once found in the island's streams are now extinct.

Eagles and falcons, though rare, can sometimes be seen soaring in the thermal currents above the mountains in search of prey, and local varieties of grouse, quail and partridge live in the fields of the interior. The migratory birds already mentioned are sometimes seen along the coasts, where the purple swamp hen has been re-introduced.

In Sicily most homes were in towns, not amidst farms. Typically these were stone row houses. Every day, farmers hiked out to the fields or orchards they cultivated. The exceptions were isolated "farm houses" or the occasional *baglio* (bailey) for lodging when a farm was especially distant from a town or village. The English and French concepts of a rural estate, with its own manor house, church and tiny hamlet, rarely applied to Sicily.

Culinary History

Even today, there are essentially two kinds of communities among the numerous towns and cities of Sicily. Inland towns, especially those in the mountains, are in the vast majority, and in the agrarian past their economies were usually based on livestock and agriculture. The economies of coastal towns were based more on fishing, commerce and maritime trade, though agriculture also contributed to their prosperity.

These factors obviously influenced the cuisine, customs and, to some extent, the mentalities of the inhabitants of these places. Until the twentieth century, somebody who lived in Castrogiovanni (Enna), Caltanissetta or any city of the mountainous interior might rarely visit the sea or taste its fruits, but plenty of goat, lamb, pork, chicken and rabbit was available. Incredible as it may seem, somebody born and raised in Centuripe might never see a roasted squid, cuttlefish or prawn.

The fact that Italy has a greater diversity of flora than any other country in western Europe has certainly influenced its cuisine, which is nothing if not regional. Piedmont is known for its risotto, Lombardy for its polenta and the southern regions for pasta.

The vegetation of Sicily is remarkably varied. Apart from the great variety of agricultural produce — ranging from citrus fruits to grapes, olives to artichokes, pistachios to mulberries, watermelon, nuts and even truffles — numerous trees, flowering shrubs and grasses are native to Sicily, though the cactus is an American import. Oleasters will still be found, along with tender wild asparagus, cardoons and even the manna ash.

Sicily's recorded culinary history dates from Greek and

Roman times. Ovid, for example, wrote about the "sweet mullet and tender eel" to be fished in Ionian waters. Pliny the Elder mentioned the lamprey as well as wine from the Etna region, local bread, delicious capers, and Sicilian cheese made from the milk of goats. Wheat, of course, was also cultivated in antiquity.

Plato mentions the lavish cuisine of Syracuse but also the excessive eating of the Syracusans. Archestratus, a Siceliot of Gela, wrote *Life of Luxury,* or *Gastronomy,* a poem dedicated to food and one of the earliest descriptions of ancient cookery.

Lentils were known to the Phoenicians and Greeks, and perhaps the indigenous Sicanians. Such simple recipes as olive paté and *maccu* (fava bean soup) were almost certainly known to the *Siceliots,* Sicily's ancient Greeks.

Meat was a mainstay of ancient Sicilian cuisine. Sausage was made in antiquity; the Syracusan dramatist Epicharmus of Kos even wrote a play called "The Sausage." The Roman culinary writer Apicius mentions foods of this kind, and indeed many still prepared today.

When sources for Sicily's culinary history seem contradictory, it is usually because they are describing different periods, perhaps centuries apart. For example, deer and wild boar no longer roam Sicilian forests because these creatures have been hunted to extinction, and in the event there were fewer woodlands for them by the eighteenth century than there were in the Middle Ages. Certain species of freshwater fish no longer survive because the rivers that sustained them are now mere seasonal streams. Mulberry trees are now rare, whereas formerly they were used in silk making. Most pistachios consumed in Sicily are now imported.

It is clear that the ancient Sicilians at least knew of certain foods which were no longer available by medieval times. The extensive mosaic pavements of the Roman villa "del Casale" erected outside Piazza Armerina around AD (CE) 360 depict all manner of fruits and beasts, many virtually unknown by the Middle Ages. Some, such as the purple swamp hen already mentioned, probably were not consumed, but there is a scene of Romans on horseback chasing relatively large deer. A pictorial resource from the fourteenth century is the wooden ceiling of the Barons' Hall in Palazzo Steri in Palermo.

The Greeks traded with northern India and central Asia, and the Romans with southern India, so it is likely that certain foods and spices were introduced via those routes. Pistachios, for example, were present in Sicily in ancient times, but they are native to central Asia.

It appears that medlars and pomegranates were also introduced by the Greeks, who brought both from western Asia, but the Phoenicians probably knew of these fruits as well.

Citrons originated in India or China and were probably brought to Greece by Alexander the Great following his battles in Persia and what is now Pakistan. Here we look to information provided by another student of Aristotle. In his lengthy treatise on plants, Theophrastus, "the father of botany," mentions rice and other crops grown in his time (he died in 287 BC), and it seems that some of these were once raised in Sicily but were no longer cultivated on the island by the fall of the Roman Empire in the fifth century. In that regard, Sicily would not be unique among Italian regions; the rice known as *arborio* has been grown in the Po Valley for many centuries and may have sustained Roman soldiers in Germany.

Early literary references to lentils, pistachios, almonds and citrons are found in the Torah. During the Roman period these foods were common among Mediterranean peoples.

The durum wheat favored by the Fatimids has been grown on the island since antiquity, and in the twelfth century, long before Marco Polo brought such recipes from China, the court geographer Abdullah al Idrisi described spaghetti being made at Trabia east of Palermo. Couscous, once a mainstay of the

Berber diet, is popular in Trapani, Marsala and Erice.

The Arabs introduced (or re-introduced) rice in Sicily during the tenth century, along with sophisticated canals and irrigation methods. Cotton (for paper as well as fabric) was also cultivated during that period but, like rice, it ceased to be grown in Sicily at some point after the Middle Ages. Sugar cane was raised in Sicily into the seventeenth century, when foreign sources became more economical.

Edible oranges and, primarily for silk making, mulberries were also brought by the Arabs. *Arancini* (rice balls), *caponata* (aubergine salad), *panelle* (ceci fritters) and various desserts made with cane sugar were all inspired by Arab agriculture and cuisine. The Arabs re-introduced sorbets, fruity ices and ice cream, which were Greek or Roman in origin.

By no means was the use of sugar limited to desserts. Indeed, it completely altered Sicilian cookery. There is, for example, *stemperata,* a delicious fish recipe based on an *agrodolce* (sweet and sour) sauce made from white wine vinegar, sugar and onions, thought to have originated in Arab times.

A fishing practice dating from that era, or perhaps a bit later, is the *mattanza,* a method for capturing large tuna in a series of "chambers" formed by giant nets. The head fisherman is accorded the Arabic title *raìs,* leader.

Tomatoes, potatoes, peppers and cocoa beans arrived with the Spaniards early in the sixteenth century. A local chocolate is still produced in Modica using the traditional method of the Aztecs. *Sfincione,* a kind of Sicilian pizza without cheese, has been made since that time; it is a thick bread topped with tomatoes, onions and anchovies. A Judaic origin has been claimed for a "white" *sfincione* made with anchovies.

We know little about the foods consumed by Sicily's Jews, who were expelled or christianized in 1493. The dearth of traditional pork recipes may reflect Kosher and Halal observances. It is interesting that the most popular offal recipes, for things like *milza* (spleen) and tripe, are for beef rather than pork, yet the Nebrodian swine seems to have been raised in the Middle Ages.

Some foods have been known in Sicily since time immemorial. As we have said, *Selinus* (Selinunte) takes its very name from the celery that grew wild on the site where the ancient city was built. The large "Hundred Horse Chestnut" outside Sant'Alfio on the slopes of Mount Etna is one of Europe's oldest nut trees, probably planted in the Roman era.

Many foods are seasonal. *Fritella* (or *fritedda* in Sicilian), a simple dish made from artichokes, fava beans and peas, is served in Spring; *maccu,* a soup made of fava, is served in Winter (from dried beans) but there's also a fresh version made in Spring.

The island of Pantelleria is known for its capers and Ustica for its lentils, while the Nebrodi region produces hazelnuts and truffles. Bronte is famous for its pistachios, for which the Sicilian word, *fatùk,* comes directly from Arabic.

It is generally believed, though not without scholarly contention, that the Greeks introduced olives and grapes, and hence olive oil and wine, perhaps with the first Mycenaean communities. More precisely, they brought the domesticated cultivars they preferred to the native oleasters and wild grapes.

Some Sicilian foods have particularly interesting links to religious tradition. The pomegranate, of course, is associated with Persephone, who was abducted in the Vale of Enna. The artichoke, whose English and Italian names come to us from the Arabic *kharshùff,* is native to the central Mediterranean and the cardoon is a distant cousin. But the Greek and Latin words are said to derive from *Cynara,* for the maiden who Zeus transformed into a beautiful artichoke flower. The citron is coveted by Jews as the *etrog* associated with Sukkot.

Following the expulsions and conversions of Sicily's Jews at the end of the fifteenth century, there were cases of *anousim,* former Jews, being tried for "Judaizing," something that usually involved kosher observances like the refusal to eat pork.

Until around 1700, published historical references to specific Sicilian recipes were fleeting at best, and low literacy among the general population meant that many families' recipes were never written down.

Historical chronicles might mention certain dishes, but they were bereft of recipes for them. Such realities have left us with only vague notions about the preparation of the lasagne and *scapace* made by the personal chef of Frederick II. The earliest known recipe for *caponata* is a modern one, even though the *Kitab al-Tabikh* of the thirteenth century mentions aubergine salad recipes.

Nevertheless, oral familial traditions, and the general similarity of certain recipes across Sicily, both suggest that many dishes have been with us for a very long time.

Traditions

There weren't many restaurants in Sicily before the nineteenth century. The first *osterie* and *trattorie* were oriented to the needs of medieval travellers. Most cooking was "home cooking" by definition.

Among the common folk were wives and mothers who made almost everything from scratch — bread, cheese, sauces, desserts. The *riveli,* tax rolls recorded every fifteen or twenty years upon collection of the *donativo,* a tax levied at royal whim, tell us that, contrary to common misperceptions, most rural households had at least a small patch of land — usually an orchard, vineyard or garden. While ordinary people were certainly far from affluent, with the larger estates, the *latifondi,* owned by the nobility, the widespread stereotype of "The Poor Peasant" is something of an exaggeration.

There was greater poverty among the urban populations of

Palermo, Catania and Messina, where the mass of people, a kind of proletariat, was referred to with disdain as the *popolino*. Here the *cuccagna,* a festival of free food offered every once in a while by the Crown or important nobles, was a cruel form of charity that sought to placate the masses in an age of chronic food shortages with a gesture of largesse. Typically, all manner of culinary delights would be prepared and placed on large, sturdy tables in a vast public square. At a certain moment guards would permit the hungry crowd to throng the tables.

The occasional generic distribution of uncooked food, such as flour, to crowds of poor Palermitans or Catanians also came to be known as a *cuccagna.*

In aristocratic homes were professional chefs. During the eighteenth century wealthier nobles hired French cooks, referred to in Sicily by the title *monsù,* from the French *monsieur.* This brought a few French influences to the cuisine known to aristocrats, though very little of this seems to have made its way into traditional country cookery.

Cloistered nuns were the keepers of many recipes, especially those for certain pastries. The quintessential example is the delicious marzipan made at Palermo's Martorana monastery. Girls educated at these convents who did not take vows might learn such recipes and someday prepare these pastries for their own children.

Unsweetened chocolate made its way into *riso nero,* literally "black rice," as well as "chocolate rabbit." A "baroque" caponata was made in the usual manner but with Modican chocolate sprinkled over it.

Religious feasts and *sagre,* food or harvest festivals, have given birth to many culinary traditions. Thus we have the *sfinci* of Saint Joseph's Day and *cuccìa* pudding for Saint Lucy's Day, the artichoke festival at Cerda and the cannolo festival at Piana degli Albanesi.

Wine never ceased to be popular in Sicily. The Normans even saw the island's Muslims consuming it in the eleventh century. But only following the Second World War did estate-bottled commercial wines become popular. Until then, most Sicilian wine was home-made. There was one early exception.

Visiting western Sicily in 1773, John Woodhouse, an English merchant, noted that the island's grapes and climate were similar to those of Portugal and southern Spain. Here he could produce a fortified wine similar to Port, Madeira and Sherry, for which there was an unslakeable demand in Britain. There was a pragmatic political reason for this decision; Britain's rapport with Spain was increasingly contentious, and by 1776 the two nations were fighting on opposing sides in the American Revolutionary War, so Marsala provided a good alternative to her Spanish sisters.

Before long, Marsala was being shipped as far as the United States, where it was served in the White House by President Thomas Jefferson. Competition eventually arrived from Benjamin Ingham and his nephew, Joseph Whitaker.

The Florio family also entered the fray. Vincenzo Florio's greatest contribution to the world was his method of preserving tuna in jars. Although this process was not his invention, he was one of the first to succeed at it commercially. Apart from wine, this was the first "processed" culinary product exported from Sicily, on Florio's own steamship line. Sicilian oranges also made their way across oceans.

But an orange, a jar of tuna and a bottle of wine, even if consumed together in an impromptu meal, don't constitute an entire cuisine. It was two things that brought Sicilian cookery to the world's attention.

The first, beginning in the eighteenth century, was the "grand tour" of European aristocrats like Goethe. In his *Italienische Reise* he wrote that "to have seen Italy without having seen Sicily is to not have seen Italy at all, for Sicily is the key to everything."

Beginning around 1880, the Sicilians who migrated to places like the United States brought their cuisine with them. A few established pasta factories and restaurants, but pizza really only became popular outside Italy around the middle of the twentieth century. At first, it was Sicilian *families* that popularized Sicilian cuisine in the Americas, and then in Britain, Australia and around the world.

Majolica

Traditionally, much of the tableware produced in Sicily was majolica, and it is still crafted here today. Decorative plates and vases are especially popular. The most important production centers are Caltagirone in the east and Santo Stefano di Camastra in the west, with styles ranging from medieval to baroque.

To discover the origins of Sicilian ceramic art we must look to the dawn of the island's history. The Sicanians, the most ancient identifiable Sicilian people, were making *terra cotta* objects more than three millennia ago. Their art was developed further under the conquering Phoenicians and the colonizing Greeks, with the latter predominating.

The Romans' arrival in Sicily brought a quasi-Etruscan influence to the Sicilian ceramic masters' art. In the Middle Ages, Byzantine and then Fatimid styles and techniques made their influence felt.

It was probably the thirteenth-century Spaniards of Catalonia and Aragon who first referred to colored Sicilian ceramic objects as *maiolica* because the glazing and firing techniques used to create these pieces were similar to those used on Majorca, the largest of the Balearic Islands. This was a logical choice of terms, since it was the Arabs who brought majolica to both Sicily and Spain.

One of the things that made medieval maiolica so obviously different from the *terra cotta* stoneware of the ancient Greeks was its glazing technique. The glazes used in majolica are usually viscous tin oxide colors applied over a white imprimatura ("ground").

Apart from its chemical composition, the characteristic that makes majolica different from porcelain is its relatively low firing temperature. Majolica was probably introduced into the Arab world sometime during the ninth century, around the time the Aghlabids of Tunisia conquered Sicily. This early majolica may have reflected the Arabs' attempts to reproduce Chinese (and Mongolian) porcelain; the painted white ground may have been an effort to duplicate porcelain's naturally light color. In the Mediterranean world the result, majolica, is an art that may be said to combine the best features of both *terra cotta* and porcelain.

For lengthier considerations of the cultures that melded to form Sicily's, we commend you to *The Peoples of Sicily: A Multicultural Legacy*.

CHAPTER 3

Accents

"Don't expect pomegranates from an olive tree."

— Sicilian Proverb

Have you ever attempted to duplicate the precise flavor of a certain dish, following the recipe scrupulously, but the result simply didn't taste exactly like what you remember enjoying?

The nuances that combine to form a distinctive flavor grow from a chorus of ingredients. In many recipes, the ensemble loses its unique impression if even one such element is missing. For the most part, the spices and condiments in Sicilian cookery are those found elsewhere. There are several unusual ones, like *bottarga* (see below), a dried caviar. Others, like pine nuts, are ubiquitous in Italian recipes. For the benefit of cooks and connoisseurs, we'll describe a few subtleties that are typically Sicilian. This is part practical and part historical.

Yes, we know that all of these items aren't available everywhere; this is where a visit to a specialty store might be necessary, and items like *bottarga* may even be available from online suppliers.

Basil, Mint, Parsley

More important than the variety is the fact that it be fresh, never dried or frozen. If you need it for a recipe, buy the *entire* stalk, leaves and all. If chopped and refrigerated, mint begins to darken almost immediately, so it's best left whole until you use it. The flavor of basil is best immediately after chopping. In Sicily, it's normal for a few whole basil leaves to be served atop pasta.

Bottarga

Like Passolina Raisins, the genuine article can be difficult to find outside Italy. Bottarga is dried, salted fish roe, usually from the bluefin tuna or from the much smaller *cefalo*, the flathead mullet (mugil cephalus). It is fine and granular, having the consistency of beach sand, and brownish in color.

Bottarga is also available in "block" form, essentially a piece of the dried roe sack.

If you must find it outside Italy, where the principal producers are in Sicily and Sardinia, note that mullet bottarga is sold as *karasumi* by Japanese vendors and as *avgotaraho* by Greek ones, though the product purchased from them may require additional drying to match the Italian roe.

As a condiment, it is typically sprinkled (or grated) over pasta.

Bread Crumbs

Presuming the use of "Italian" or "French" white bread, it is important to keep in mind that the bread crumbs used in

Sicilian recipes include the crust; some very "white" bread crumbs sold commercially do not. The Italian word is *mollica,* and in Sicily it sometimes refers to bread crumbs "toasted" in a frying pan with olive oil and finely-chopped garlic, used as a condiment (in place of cheese) sprinkled over certain types of pasta.

Capers

These are discussed at length elsewhere. In Sicily capers were traditionally sold dried and salted. They are green. Some capers are bottled in vinegar or salt water. It's best to buy the kind in water or vinegar. Straining, then soaking in cold water for twenty minutes, will remove traces of salt.

Honey

Known to the most ancient civilizations, honey has been produced in Sicily for thousands of years, but its flavor has changed over the centuries. This is not to suggest that the bees (the productive "Italian" variety *Apis Mellifera Ligustica* known the world over) have changed their methods. It's the flowers that have changed. In antiquity, wild flowers were the main source of nectar in Sicily, and in most other regions. The honey known in Italy as *millefiori* ("thousands of flowers") reflects this ancient heritage. Today, however, most Sicilian honey is made from orange blossom nectar or even eucalyptus nectar. Less often, the honey produced in Sicily is made from the blossoms of almonds and other trees. Bees are important for pollination; fruit production would be less were it not for the honeybee, and there is a crisis in this regard in North America.

Citrus fruits were known to the Romans, whose empire encompassed citrus-growing regions in Egypt and Persia, but it was the Arabs who introduced the widespread cultivation of lemons and oranges in Sicily in the ninth century. This profoundly influenced the composition of the nectar from which most Sicilian honey is made, for its flavor is a direct result of that of the bees' source.

But the Arabs introduced another crop, one which was to attenuate the importance of honey as a sweetener. This was sugar cane (described below). Like cotton — also introduced in Sicily by the Saracens — sugar cane is no longer raised in Sicily, yet the use of cane sugar in sweets completely changed the face of medieval Sicilian cuisine. It meant that the tasty frostings, candied fruits and cheese filling of *cassata,* and the creamy filling of *cannoli,* preparations attributed to the Sicilian Arabs, could be made with a powdered cane sugar. Sugar was sometimes used, as an alternative to simple drying, to preserve fruits. Ice cream had existed in Sicily at least since Roman times but it too would now be prepared with cane sugar. Indeed, Sicilian honey production decreased drastically following the introduction of cane sugar. By the thirteenth century, it was no longer considered an important product and beekeepers were few.

This explains why so few existing Sicilian recipes call for honey as an essential ingredient. Sicilian cuisine is not unique in this regard. The increasingly widespread use of cane sugar reduced honey's importance in many parts of the world, forcing local cuisines to evolve in unexpected ways. Most of the Sicilian confections enjoyed today were handed down to us from the Arabs who ruled the island for three centuries until the Normans arrived. There has been a slight resurgence of honey production in Sicily in recent years. Quantities are small but quality is high.

"Varietal" honey (made from one kind of flower) seems to be the current rage, and Sicilian Orange Blossom is the quintessentially Sicilian flavor.

Mushrooms

Several edible, wild Sicilian varieties grow in the woods of the Madonie and Nebrodi Mountains.

Nuts (Pine nuts, Almonds, Pistachios)

These should not be toasted unless specified by the recipe, and never salted. Sicilian almonds and pistachios are discussed later. Sicilian pine nuts are usually larger than those sold elsewhere in Italy.

Olives and Olive Oil

This is considered in detail in a later chapter. What is important is that the oil be a high-quality, extra virgin oil, preferably unfiltered. This is a formal classification. There are some Greek and Spanish olive varieties that can substitute for Sicilian ones.

Raisins (Passolina)

A number of Sicilian recipes call for a small, sweet raisin rare outside Sicily, Calabria and Sardinia. Most often, it is golden in color, made from a golden grape called (generically) the Sultanina, but a darker variety, the tiny Passolina, is usually made from the Corinto grape. In the United States, a grape variety very similar to the Sultanina is the Thompson Seedless — only rarely are seedless grapes cultivated in Sicily.

Italian raisin production is surprisingly limited if we consider that it is the European nation that produces more grapes than any other. Many of the raisins consumed in Italy are imported from Turkey.

True Sicilian Passolinas are rarely available outside Sicily.

Here the best advice, if a substitution is contemplated, is to find the smallest, naturally-sweet raisins available.

Ricotta

This is described in the cheese chapter. In Sicily *ricotta* is made from sheep's milk. If that's not available, choose the best, finely-textured, whole-milk *ricotta* you can find, never generic "cottage cheese."

Saffron

This is a deep yellow powder taken from the dried stigmas of a flower, *crocus sativus*, which blossoms red or purple. Saffron was probably introduced in Sicily by the Arabs, although the Greeks seem to have known of it. It is used in rice balls and sometimes in pasta with sardines.

Sea Salt

Trapani and Marsala are famous for more than wine and seafood. Trapani, in particular, boasts some of Europe's oldest salt marshes, and is still home to some of the windmills once used to drain water from the basins (containing ponds). Drawing salt from water remains a slow process, similar to desalination, something talked about more and more with the water supply problems confronting Sicily. The evaporation procedure utilizes the flat marshlands of Trapani's coast and the long, dry Sicilian summers.

Salt extraction was a technology known to the ancient Egyptians, and in Sicily dates at least from the time of the Greeks and Romans. The phrase "worth his salt" alludes to the practice of the Roman generals paying their soldiers in salt rather than coinage. Salt extraction has flourished in the Trapani area unto the present day, not for a lack of "dry" salt deposits in Sicily (where there are several mines), but because many cooks prefer sea salt to that harvested from other sources. The windmills, however, were a medieval development.

By the nineteenth century, Sicilian sea salt was exported to European countries as far away as Norway and Russia. Several of the British firms involved in other Sicilian exports, namely Marsala wine and sulfur, helped to develop the international trade in sea salt.

In Sicily, the sea salt is often sold wet or damp. For this reason a few grains of rice are sometimes placed with the salt in a shaker to absorb moisture and to prevent caking.

Trapani, ancient Drepanum, was the port for Erice, and the town's fortunes have always been tied to the sea. By the nineteenth century tuna had become an important product. It still is. Salt is just one part of the picture.

Nobody doubts the purity of Trapani's salt, but its trace elements give it a special flavor. It seems perfect for fish recipes like the seafood couscous for which Trapani is famous. The windmills are no longer necessary, but at least a few continue to turn, and tourists enjoy visiting them.

Sugar Cane

Sicily no longer produces sugar, so our observations here are primarily historical.

Saccharum officinarum (loosely translated "noble cane") probably originated in Polynesia, to be introduced in India and China in antiquity, though some genetic research suggests a mainland Asian origin. The Persians were producing sugar from cane by 500 BC (BCE), if not earlier. With the Arab invasion of Persia in 642, rudimentary sugar cane refining techniques were acquired by eastern Mediterranean peoples.

By 900, the cane was being grown in Arab Sicily, one of the few European regions where this tropical plant has ever been cultivated. Sugar cane needs a humid, tropical climate, with plenty of precipitation (or irrigation).

The Arabs were experts at designing efficient irrigation systems, and in the tenth century Sicily had more rivers and natural lakes — and more rain — than it does today. Broadly classified as a perennial grass, sugar cane grows to a height of over three meters (ten feet). Notwithstanding superior irrigation methods, sugar cane usually was grown in Sicily's flat coastal areas, which in the Middle Ages were often marshy, particularly near Catania, Marsala and Trapani.

Some sugar cane grows wild in Sicily today, though most of the tall, reed-like cane plants one sees growing near streams are not sugar cane.

The great advantage of sugar as a sweetener was that, unlike honey, it did not have a strong, overpowering flavor of its own.

Truffles

Very few Sicilian recipes call for these but, like wild mushrooms, they grow in the forests of the Nebrodi and Madonie Mountains. (See the next chapter.)

Wines

Like olive oil, wines are dealt with in detail later. At the outset, let's agree on at least one point. In cooking, there is absolutely no substitute for genuine Sicilian Marsala. Never.

In planning a Sicilian meal, Sicilian wines are recommended whenever possible. Chardonnay is a poor substitute for Cataratto, and Syrah cannot match Nero d'Avola.

CHAPTER 4

Fruits and Vegetables

"Caronia possesses gardens, springs, vineyards and fruit trees. It boasts a fine port where fishermen set up nets to capture large tuna."

— Idrisi, *The Book of King Roger*

By longstanding tradition, it was the fruits of the land that formed the foundation of Sicilian cuisine and what has come to be known in recent decades as the Mediterranean Diet. Depending on the times, meats and fish, though included in most diets, might be seen as luxuries.

In this book we focus on distinctively "Sicilian" fruits and vegetables, things that make Sicilian cuisine *Sicilian,* with apologies to arugula and the humble tomato. Olives have their own chapter, while mushrooms were mentioned in the previous one.

Whilst bearing in mind that most of our readers live *outside* Italy, it seems appropriate, for completeness, to begin by explaining, if only succinctly, where in Sicily one purchases these items.

Sicilian Street Markets

A Sicilian street market is a cacophony of sights and sounds, from a colorful assortment of fruits, vegetables, fish and meats to vendors barking about bargains for anybody who will listen. The ambience is punctuated by colored tarpaulins suspended as "tents" to protect the wares from the elements. Italian and foreign items vie for your attention: *tarocchi* (blood oranges), *giri* (leafy chards), chicory, herbs, artichokes, cuttlefish, swordfish, prawns, cheeses, olives, gutted goats and lambs. And that's just the beginning.

Sicily's outdoor market tradition dates from the ninth-century Saracen rule of the island, which explains their striking similarity to Arab *souqs*. Even some of their names are Arabic in origin; Palermo's *Ballarò* comes to mind. The weather helps. Outdoor vendors find a pleasant environment in coastal cities where it hardly ever gets cold enough to snow. That's not to say that Sicily's markets will be found only in the largest cities. Almost every town and urban neighbourhood has its *mercatino* ("little market") open once or twice a week.

Especially in the Arabs' beloved Bal'harm (today's Palermo), where the open air markets occupy narrow medieval streets and the local dialect bears the marks of the Arabic tongue, the visitor might be forgiven for thinking that she has wandered into an old quarter in Cairo, Tunis, Jerusalem or Baghdad. Here in Sicily's markets, there are more churches and fewer mosques, more miniskirts and fewer veils, but the character has remained essentially the same over these last nine centuries. That's remarkable if you consider that a few of the outdoor markets stand on the very same sites today as they did in the tenth century. With the exception of some Norman-Arab architecture and a number of words in the Sicilian language, the markets are perhaps the best-preserved of Sicily's Fatimid traditions. Following in the footsteps of their medieval predecessors, Sicily's new North African immigrants — a growing presence — feel perfectly at home here, and are beginning to establish businesses.

In Catania, so frequently the prey of earthquakes and volcanic eruptions, the architecture is more open, the historical quarters having been largely rebuilt. Here in eastern Sicily's main city the markets are located not in narrow medieval streets but in open Baroque squares. The largest is in Piazza Carlo Alberto, flanked by picturesque churches and monasteries. Another, located near the cathedral, is part of a vast fish market, now expanded to sell just about everything. It's a gastronome's delight. In comparing the Palermitan and Catanian markets, one is struck by the greater variety of seafood and produce available in the latter. Catania's markets sell more kinds of artichoke, mushroom and broccoli than you'll find in Palermo. The Carlo Alberto market, in particular, sells more foods, like cheeses and salad ingredients, that are ready to eat.

Late on weekday afternoons, trays and cauldrons appear with food ready to take home and eat for supper.

The open air markets are a great place to soak up some local atmosphere even if you don't actually buy anything. You'll have to know where to find them, hidden as they are from the main streets. Siracusa, Messina, Trapani and other major Sicilian cities also boast large markets, but nothing as extensive as those in Palermo and Catania. Here's a simple guide to Sicily's five largest outdoor markets in Sicily's two largest cities.

In Palermo: Located a few steps from the Martorana Church and Quattro Canti, the *Ballarò* market extends from Piazza Ballarò in the Albergheria district (near the church of San Nicolò) along Via Ballarò past Piazza Carmine toward Corso Tukory, roughly parallel to Via Maqueda toward the main train station. The *Capo* market, located behind the Teatro Massimo, extends from Via Porta Carini off Via Volturno near the old city wall toward Piazza Beati Paoli and can also be reached from Via Sant'Agostino, which runs off Via Maqueda, though this section includes various vendors of dry goods and articles other than food. *Vucciria* (from the Norman French *boucherie*), once the favorite Palermitan market for visitors, begins at Piazza San Domenico, off Via Roma, running parallel to Via Roma (from which it is hidden) along Via Maccheronai toward Piazza Caracciolo and Corso Vittorio Emanuele, branching off along Via Argenteria. Palermo's markets are usually open all day (from around nine to seven) except Wednesday, when they close around two in the afternoon, and the two larger ones, *Capo* and *Ballarò,* are partly open Sunday mornings.

In Catania: The *Piazza Carlo Alberto* market is located in a large square (named for one of the nineteenth-century Piedmontese kings) near Via Umberto and Corso Sicilia, easily reached from Via Pacini off Via Etnea near the Villa Bellini park. The *Pescheria* ("fish market") is located off Piazza Duomo near the cathedral and fountain "dell'Amenano" between Via Garibaldi and Via Pacini, extending along Via Gemelli Zappalà and some of the nearby streets. Catania's markets are closed Sundays and some afternoons.

Almonds

First cultivated in the Middle East, the almond was probably introduced in Sicily before 1000 BC (BCE). There are several varieties of almond (including bitter and sweet almonds), all related to *prunus amygdalus.* The idea that sweet almonds grow from white flowers and bitter ones from pinkish blossoms is somewhat misleading, at least in Sicily. The almond, which is related to the peach and plum, is the pit (stone) of a green husk. Indeed, the almond shell and seed (kernel) resemble those of the peach — also widely cultivated in Sicily. In addition to the almond nuts themselves, the seeds yield a tasty oil and certain potentially toxic substances (the cyanides). Almonds are rich in Vitamin E and are a good source of healthy monounsaturated fats.

In the Bible the almond is variously referred to as *shakked* and *luz* (the latter also refers to hazels). The Latin for almond is *amygdalus* (from the Greek *amugdale*), which in medieval times became *amandolus.* The Old French, from which the English word comes, was *almande,* and the Italian word is *mandorlo.* The Sicilian word was *mandola* or *mendula.*

In southern Sicily almonds blossom as early as January, and in February Agrigento celebrates its Almond Blossom Festival.

There are numerous Biblical (Old Testament) references to almond trees, which early in history became symbolic of various virtues and myths. Anciently almonds were cultivated across southern Eurasia, from Spain to Turkey to India to China, and today they are widely grown in the Americas. Today Italy is one of the major producers of almonds, surpassed by several nations. Almonds are the world's most widely grown and consumed tree nut.

The almond tree grows to a height of about ten metres (thirty feet). After olive trees, almond trees are the most widely cultivated fruit tree in Sicily, where there are various, subtly-distinguished varieties. In Roman times, almonds were cultivated as far north as Normandy and southern England, but the trees rarely survive a hard freeze, and they produce less fruit in cooler regions (northern Europe was probably slightly warmer two thousand years ago). Sicilian almonds are harvested in July, if not earlier. Very few find their way into the export market. Most Sicilian almonds, like Sicilian pistachios, are used in confections, though some are used to make sweet liqueur and even almond-flavored wines, thought to be an aphrodisiac.

Almonds symbolize good fortune, and as sugar-coated *confetti* they are given at Italian weddings and baptisms. This custom has become international. (The term *confetti* used to describe bits of multicolored paper is properly *coriandoli* in Italian.)

In Sicily the association of the almond tree with love and fidelity is rooted in Greek mythology. Phyllis, a noble maiden, wed Demophon, who visited Thrace to wed her after the Trojan War but then departed. Phyllis waited for him to return, but after some years died of a broken heart. An almond tree sprang up at her grave. The tree finally bloomed when Demophon visited the grave of his beloved wife. In Judaic history, Samson presented flowering almond branches to attract Delilah.

Artichokes

A longstanding theory suggests that artichokes actually originated in Sicily. That would be a unique distinction in a land whose culture and cuisine is an amalgamation of foreign ones. In any event, we know that the globe artichoke, *cynara scolymus,* cultivated in some fifty varieties, evolved in the western or central Mediterranean. Artichokes are in the *asteraceae* (or compositae) family. The purplish wild, spiny artichoke, featuring tough leaves ending in thorns, is the most popular form in Sicily, where one town, Cerda, has erected a tall sculptural monument to this most singular vegetable in the main square.

This thistle-like perennial should not be confused with the Jerusalem artichoke, related to the sunflower. More closely related to the artichoke is its country cousin, the cardoon, *cynara cardunculus,* a delicacy whose comparatively slender stalks are harvested in late Autumn. Sicilians, however, make little distinction here, and sometimes consume the thicker stalks of the artichoke as though they were, in fact, cardoons. The buds of the true cardoon (known as *carduna* to Sicilians) are not usually eaten, while those of *scolymus* are consumed as artichokes. Cardoons are taller than artichoke plants, which grow closer to the ground. Some artichokes are quite large, and range in color from deep green to yellowish or even purplish. Most domesticated varieties have no thorns.

The artichoke was known in Norman Sicily and Moorish Spain, though it appears not to have been very widely cultivated in mainland Italy during that period. This suggests an Arab origin. The Latin word is *cynara,* while the Italian word *carciofo* is a cognate of the Arabic *kharshuff.* In Sicily, Greek and Roman artistic representations of the purple flower suggest that the species was present centuries before the medieval Saracen conquest of the island. The literary works of Pliny and other ancient writers associated with Greece and Sicily suggest that little distinction was made between the artichoke and the cardoon, and this is consistent with occasional Sicilian usage. Artichokes, which don't need too much moisture, are harvested twice annually, beginning as early as March. The Spring harvest is more substantial than the Autumn crop.

They're not the foundation of any diet, but artichokes are a good source of ascorbic acid (Vitamin C), niacin, magnesium, potassium, iron, copper, phosphorus, calcium and fiber. The substance *cynarin* is thought to benefit digestion, while the juice of the leaves is used in skin cosmetics. An artichoke liqueur bearing the trade name *Cynar* is made in Sicily. Artichokes can be prepared in many ways. As well as the heart, the soft inner leaves can be eaten if cooked well. Most of the world's artichokes are produced in Italy, where Sardinia rivals Sicily for quantity. Until recently, artichokes were regarded as an esoteric specialty food by many people beyond the Mediterranean region. No more. With fava beans, the artichoke is an important ingredient of fritella (fritedda), a Spring dish in Sicily.

Spanish settlers introduced the artichoke to the New World as early as the seventeenth century, and Italian immigrants began the cultivation of other varieties in California during the twentieth century. To the ancient Romans, the artichoke was believed to be an aphrodisiac, identified with the myth of Cynara. Artichoke festivals are not unique to Sicily. Marilyn Monroe was once crowned Artichoke Queen of a Californian town.

Asparagus

There was a time, before the age of hybrid crops, genetic engineering and "agribusiness," when many fruits and vegetables tasted better. "Wild" salmon and mussels were fished from the seas, not harvested from "farms." Rabbit and hare were hunted, not "raised." Livestock wasn't "beefed up" with hormones. And flavors were different. The good news is that a few of these untamed flavors still exist, and Sicily's wild asparagus offers one of them. This rare delight is picked each Spring in the mountains of Sicily. Like *carduna* and wild thorny artichokes, it's something you'll rarely find outside southern Italy or a few other parts of the Mediterranean.

Wild *asparagus acutifolius* is a country cousin of *asparagus officinalis,* the common domesticated variety, which has a thicker stalk and sweeter taste. It may even be accurate to refer to wild asparagus as an uncle or aunt of *officinalis,* but we'll leave that debate to the botanical geneticists. Truth be told, wild asparagus, a perennial, is sometimes grown on farms, but its flavor does not seem to have suffered much for the change of scenery.

The sweeter, tender "domesticated" asparagus is raised in Sicily and sold in supermarkets. To find wild asparagus you'll probably have to venture into one of Sicily's outdoor street markets during April or early May.

In Sicily the word *sparacelli* is still used in most regions to refer to wild asparagus, though in the western part of the island *sparacelli* also refers to wild broccoli. Asparagus, in one form or another, is native to many areas around the world. It is the stalks and buds that are eaten, as the sprouts are picked before they flower. Wild Sicilian asparagus has slender, slightly purplish stalks and a rather bitter taste compared to the more common supermarket variety.

Asparagus, which is a diuretic, was cultivated by the ancient Egyptians, Greeks and Romans, and a recipe survives from the compilation by Apicius. Low in sodium, asparagus is a good source of several minerals, including magnesium, calcium, and zinc, as well as folic acid, vitamins A, C, E and K, and iron, selenium and potassium.

Asparagine, an amino acid, takes its name from asparagus, and is cognate to the Sicilian word *sparacelli*. The Latin word is *sparagus,* from the Greek *asparagos*. The Persian *asparag* meant "sprout" or "shoot."

Asparagus is not the kind of vegetable most of us prefer to eat raw. Wild Sicilian asparagus is tougher than other varieties to begin with, so boiling or steaming is recommended. It's great in a *frittata,* with sharp *caciocavallo* cheese.

Aubergines

This is the eggplant, which is mentioned in a Chinese text written during the sixth century.

Aubergines (Solanum Melongena) seem to have been unknown to the ancient Romans. Domesticated for millennia, the eggplant is native to Asia. It was introduced in the Mediterranean region by the Arabs in their rapid expansion ever westward. The Italian word is *melanzana*.

The quintessential Sicilian eggplant recipe is caponata, a salad of aubergines, olives and capers.

Broccoli and Sparacelli

Early Spring is the time to enjoy Sicily's "winter harvest." Artichokes and fava beans — two essential ingredients of fritella — top the list. Then there's broccoli.

Few vegetables have such a bad reputation with children, perhaps because of mothers' lack of creativity in preparing broccoli.

Thought to be indigenous to Italy, broccoli is but one cultivar in the *Brassica oleracea* group, which also includes cabbages and cauliflower. *Purple broccoli* should not be confused with *violet cauliflower,* which is white with deep purple accents, while *Romanesco* "broccoli" ("broccoflower") is actually a greenish cauliflower. There is, in fact, a distinct difference between broccoli, whose firm green stalks end in florets having looser buds, and cauliflower, whose soft, thick, whitish, tuber-like stalks form a dense, roundish mass ending in clumped buds.

Broccoli was cultivated by the ancient Romans, derived from the wild *broccolo.* This quasi-domesticated vegetable is what is often sold in western Sicily — particularly around Palermo — as *sparacelli,* a word which elsewhere on the island refers to wild Sicilian asparagus (see above). Sparacelli sometimes has a bluish cast, but not nearly as much as purple broccoli, and its buds are larger and more separated than those of the generic "Calabrian" broccoli. In general, the heads of the sparacelli broccolo are much smaller than those of Calabrian broccoli.

Calabrian broccoli is the more refined vegetable sold around the world. It has a large, bulbous head similar to that of purple broccoli but usually has a deeper green color.

Broccoli aficionados and fanatics, of which there are a few, insist on the wild broccolo (sparacelli) which, compared to Calabrian broccoli, is rather tough to eat raw — especially for those who enjoy the leaves and stems as well as the florets.

Cima di rapa (rapini) resembles broccoli, and bears a similarity of flavor, but is in the mustard family.

Broccoli is full of vitamins A, C and K, as well as several B vitamins, minerals and antioxidants, as well as dietary fibre. In the recipe chapter you'll find two great Sicilian ways to enjoy it.

Capers

Capers are grown in southern Italy, but particularly on the island of Pantelleria off the Sicilian coast. It's a perpetually windy island, where the olive trees are pruned to a squat form to survive heavy gusts, and the perfect place for caper plants, which grow close to the ground. The plant, *capparis spinosa,* belongs to the family *capparidaceae.* There are various varieties of caper, particularly in central Asia and India.

It is believed that capers originated in western or central Asia, though it has also been suggested that capparis spinosa is native to the Mediterranean Basin, which encompasses the Black Sea and other regions touching western Asia. The Roman author Pliny the Elder, who wrote about Sicilian cuisine, mentioned capers, and so did ancient Greeks. Capers similar to those of Pantelleria grow in many Mediterranean countries.

The caper itself is the bud of a flowering plant, and the stage at which the buds are harvested is very important. Some caper buds sold for the culinary market are quite large, reaching over two centimeters (almost an inch) in diameter, though most are much smaller.

Capers' strong, distinctive flavor comes from mustard oil. Capers are high in rutin, but are usually consumed only as an enhancement. In Sicilian cuisine, the eggplant (aubergine) salad known as caponata is made with capers. They are often sold either salted or in vinegar or brine. To eliminate these other flavors, it is usually best to soak capers in cold water and strain before serving.

Cultivation and harvesting is labor-intensive, having changed little in centuries. The "caper berries" are harvested from plants which rarely reach a meter in height. As the buds are picked before blossoming, caper flowers are a rare sight. In some regions, however, capers grow wild.

Strongly identified with Italian cuisine, capers are also cultivated on a large scale in Spain. It was the Spaniards who introduced capers in the Americas. In fact, Pantelleria is one of the few Italian regions where capers are still grown, though capers are also raised in the Aeolian Islands off the Sicilian coast near Messina. Cyprus, Greece, Dalmatia, Provence and Morocco are also known for caper production.

Capers are not as prevalent in Sicilian cuisine as one might expect, but creative uses abound. Potato ("Russian") salad, for example, may be enhanced with a few capers, while the buds make an appealing garnish for many dishes. A swordfish recipe popular in Messina calls for capers.

Caper blossoms are edible. These are *cucunci*. The mature caper fruit — as opposed to the buds — can reach the size of a large olive.

Capers are one of the things that make life more pleasant.

Cardoons

It is a verity of culinary history that a local cuisine is based on things which were indigenous to the local environment. But traditional foods can be influenced by foreign imports. People don't always realize that tomatoes, peppers and other features of modern Italian cuisine began their history as foods far away (in those cases the Americas). Only since the Middle Ages have certain crops been introduced beyond their places of origin.

The *cardoon* has done less wandering than its better-known cousin, the more aristocratic artichoke. Yet thistles similar to the cardoon grow wild around the world — the thistle flower is the traditional symbol of Scotland. Sicily just happens to be one of the few places where the stalks of certain types of thistle are consumed. Here the dish is called *carduna,* from the Latin term *carduus* (which is the plant's principal genus). The Italian word *cardo* is more generic and does not refer to a specific scientific family; in North America certain types of thistle are similar to the cardoon and some are the same varieties, having been introduced into Mexico and California by the Spaniards. Thistles have prickly stems and leaves and rounded heads of purple, violet or pinkish flowers. They are related to certain kinds of daisies.

The cardoon, "artichoke thistle" or "musk thistle," is in the *asteraceae* family. Its stalks are similar to those of the artichoke — another thistle in the *asteraceae* family indigenous to Sicily — and have a similar taste and texture. Only in the eighteenth century were these plants identified scientifically, though they had obviously been consumed for millennia. The cardoon is mentioned anciently in Egypt and Ethiopia, and makes an appearance in both Greek and Norse mythology.

The cardoon most often consumed in Sicily is the *cynara cardunculus,* which is indeed closely related to the artichoke, *cynara scolymus.* The leaves and stalks of the two plants are nearly identical; it's the flowers that are different. Artichokes are harvested in late autumn and again in early spring, but the cardoon stalk is usually picked once annually, beginning in early December.

Bearing a vague resemblance to celery, the cardoon stalk is high in potassium, low in sodium, and is a good source of B vitamins, folate, magnesium, calcium and iron. For all its nutritional benefit and delicious taste, the cardoon enjoys little more than a cult following among gourmands and aficionados beyond the Mediterranean. It seems to be regarded as the "poor cousin" of the more famous artichoke.

Genuine cardoons don't grow everywhere. In North America and parts of northern Europe it may be possible to substitute certain wild thistle stalks for cardoons. These may be tougher and therefore require longer boiling during preparation, for 15 or 20 minutes. They may also be thinner, yet probably not much more bitter than the true cardoon. Yes, cardoon stalks are rather bitter.

Preparation for cooking begins with cutting the long stalks and removing some of the tough external fibres. Next the stalks are boiled (with a little salt) in a large pot for at least ten minutes. This is the cooking stage, and if you prefer you can eat the stalks this way, but in Sicily the carduna is rarely served after having been merely boiled. Instead, it is then lightly battered (dipped in whole egg, dredged through flour and then perhaps rolled in bread crumbs with a bit of pepper and finely grated cheese) and quickly fried. A heavy, pasty batter should not be used, and the cardoons should not be deep fried, but quickly pan fried in a mixture of corn oil and refined olive oil.

Carduna is served simply, without dressings or dips. Tasting it with a bit of horseradish or wasabi sauce, or even Dijon mustard, while not grounds for trial on heresy charges, is less than traditional. Sicilians prefer — if anything — a generous splash of fresh lemon juice.

Chestnuts

The days can be quite warm in Sicily well into October, but the first nights of the month are usually relatively cool, even in the largest cities. That's when you'll begin to see chestnut vendors roasting the annual harvest of *castagne* from the Nebrodi and Madonie mountains or the slopes of Etna. Chestnuts are the quintessential street food, and here in Sicily they are roasted in what look like wide, long iron pipes. The result is a thoroughly cooked, slightly charred chestnut dusted in a greyish ash.

In Catania and Palermo you'll see the white smoke wafting into the crisp evening air in busier squares from October through March. Hardly anybody roasts them at home.

Chestnuts are regarded as a European food popularized during the Middle Ages. Related to the oak and the beech, the genus *castanea* is Eurasian and North American. Edible European varieties are of the so-called *sweet chestnut* (castanea sativa), introduced in antiquity from Asia Minor, probably by prehistoric neolithic farmers. The ancient Greeks and Romans subsequently introduced them over a wider range of cultivation, extending into Britain and northeastern Gaul (France). Its hard wood is highly prized, and chestnut trees seem to live forever.

One of the oldest trees in Europe is a chestnut tree in eastern Sicily, the Hundred Horse Chestnut outside Sant'Alfio in the Etna region, estimated to be well over two thousand years old. It is certainly the oldest in Italy, its documented history dating from the fifteenth century, and it also happens to be one of the largest (widest) trees in Europe. However, Italy's principal chestnut-growing region ranges from Mugello in Tuscany northward into Liguria and Piedmont. Almonds and hazelnuts are far more common in Sicilian cuisine nowadays; chestnut flour, formerly popular in making a certain kind of Sicilian bread, is rare in Sicilian cookery.

Castagno, Castagnaro, Castagnolo and various Sicilian surnames reflect the profession of "chestnut grower" and it appears that there were far more chestnut trees in Sicily a few centuries ago than there are today. There were also more oaks, though truffles are still found in the Nebrodi region. However, the term *castano* also refers to the color brown or reddish "chestnut" brown. A chestnut orchard is a *castagneto* or (in Sicilian) a *castagnitu*. In the Etna region, not too far from the ancient chestnut tree, is a town called *Trecastagni* (literally "three chestnut trees").

Chestnuts are rich in various minerals, especially potassium, phosphorus, magnesium and calcium. Unlike most nuts, they contain a substantial quantity of ascorbic acid (Vitamin C). They can, in theory, be eaten raw.

Oddly enough, while *marrons glacé* are considered something of a luxury today, chestnuts were historically viewed as poor food for poor people. That image seems to be changing.

Chickpeas

It was a violent event that ushered the humble chickpea (ceci) into the annals of Sicilian history.

In 1282, a conspiracy and mass riot subsequently known as the War of the Vespers led to the expulsion of the Angevin French from Sicily. By this time, the "native" nobility, for the most part descended from Normans, Germans, Lombards and Byzantines, spoke an early dialect of Sicilian.

On the other hand, most of the Angevins enfeoffed since the defeat of the heirs of Frederick II some fifteen years earlier spoke French among themselves. When these conquerors did speak Sicilian or Italian, it was with a strong French accent, yet they didn't look any different from the native nobles.

To identify them, the leading revolutionaries demanded that one Frenchman after another pronounce the word for a chick pea. Perhaps they held up a bean to be identified by name. The French, so the chronicles tell us, pronounced *ciciri* with a very distinct — and very foreign — accent and were killed.

Chickpeas (or garbanzos) were probably introduced in Sicily in neolithic times by peoples arriving from the eastern Mediterranean during our island's "Proto-Sicanian" period.

Originating in western Asia, the legume *Fabaceae Cicer Arietinum* found its way into the cuisine of cultures ranging from what is now Portugal to present-day China. Across this wide section of Asia, Africa and Europe, domesticated chickpeas dated as early as 6000 BC (BCE) have been found at archeological sites and caves. At sites in Turkey and Israel they have been found in pottery of the Late Neolithic, circa 3500 BC.

In their love of the chickpea, the Greeks and Romans were merely following in the footsteps of earlier civilizations, and ceci foods have been found at Roman sites across Europe. The surname *Cicero* derives from a Latin word denoting the profession of ceci farmer. For their presumed medicinal and fertility properties, chickpeas were associated with the goddess Venus.

In Sicily, chickpea flour is the main ingredient in *panella*. In the Middle East, it is used to make hummus and (with fava beans) falafels. *Desi* chickpeas are ubiquitous in Indian cuisine; in Sicily the variety is the *kabuli,* and in Puglia black chickpeas are cultivated. Historically, chickpeas were dried for preservation. Toasted chickpeas are still part of Sicilian cuisine after many centuries.

High in fiber, vitamins and minerals — especially folate, zinc, iron, magnesium, calcium, phosphorus and potassium — chickpeas are a particularly healthy food. Some studies have even indicated that they may help to lower cholesterol in the bloodstream.

A very beneficial food, even if you wouldn't be able to pronounce its Sicilian name correctly to save your life.

Citron

The dignified citron suffers a perpetual identity crisis, almost a kind of botanical identity theft inflicted by its distant cousin, the humble lemon. So far as we can tell, there seem to be two reasons for this. In certain languages, such as French, *citron* refers to the lemon, while the fruit of certain citron varieties resembles a lemon and has a rather similar taste. In French, citron is *cédrat*. The citron is viewed by many as eccentric, even esoteric. But not in Sicily.

The fruit is mostly a thick, white rind. This, as well as the juicy pulp (flesh) and skin (peel), are edible. The skin, in particular, is often used in baking. The citron has a bitter taste. The sugared rind is known as *succade*.

The geographical origin of *citrus medica* (citron's official name) during historic times is uncertain, though India and Yemen are often suggested. In fact, all citrus species probably originated in southeast Asia long ago. In antiquity citron was used medicinally as a cure for seasickness and other ailments, and sometimes as an antidote to certain poisons. It is a good source of soluble fiber. In Persia it was traditionally used to make jam, and in India citron is chopped and pickled in preserves. The Koreans make citron tea.

As the *etrog* (its Hebrew name), the citron is used ritually by Jews at Taberna (the Feast of the Tabernacles during Sukkot). According to the Torah, the Jews brought the fruit with them during the Exodus, and indeed ancient Egyptian art depicts the citron. There exists a theory that the citron was the forbidden fruit of the Garden of Eden.

Citron was probably introduced in Sicily during the Greek or Roman periods, and figures such as Alexander the Great are sometimes identified as having brought it westward. Pliny the Elder writes of it. In mosaics and other works of art of the ancient era the yellow fruits sometimes identified as lemons are actually citrons. Lemons and oranges, though known to the Romans, were first widely cultivated in Sicily by the Arabs. Citron seeds uncovered in Mesopotamian excavations date from circa 4000 BC (BCE). It was probably the Spaniards who brought the domesticated fruit to the New World.

There are various varieties of citron. When ripe, the citron fruit is deep yellow in color, almost orange. The variety most widely cultivated in Sicily is the *diamante*. In Sicily the citron is usually propagated from cuttings rather than seeds, so most trees are "clones." The trees usually begin to bear fruit after around five years.

Like the lemon, the citron bears fruit several times during the year. It is, of course, cultivated on warmer climates where the ground never freezes. This includes most of Sicily. The tree grows to a height of almost five meters (16 feet). The oval fruit, which is very fragrant, varies in size, easily reaching 25 centimetres (10 inches) in length.

The citron is thought to be one of the oldest "pure" citrus species, along with the mandarin orange, papeda and pummelo. The various "domesticated" orange and lemon varieties, on the other hand, developed through random hybridisation over many millennia. The citron, which self pollinates, is probably the oldest of all these fruits. In neolithic times it was probably more widely cultivated than either the lemon or the orange. It is probable that the citron was displaced by the lemon over time because the latter is easier to grow and, of course, juicier.

Candied citron is popular in confectionary, often mixed in tiny pieces into cannolo cream or used to decorate frosted cassata cakes. Citron preserves are similar to *cucuzzata,* or *zuccata,* sweetened squash preserves.

Perhaps it was destiny that this most unusual fruit was meant to be appreciated most by God's Chosen People.

Fava Beans

Picture this. You're at a bar in Sicily where you order bitters, champagne or one of those other drinks they serve with "munchies" like olives, peanuts or potato crisps. One of the enticing snacks looks a little like reddish barbecued potato chips, only thicker and a bit smaller. Salty and spicy, they have a robust flavor but at first you can't quite figure out what they are. Then it dawns on you. You're eating toasted *fava beans* (broad beans) flavored with paprika.

It's a Sicilian thing. Like other typically Sicilian crops, fava beans — scientifically known as *vicia faba* — were introduced on the island in the remote past, perhaps by the Phoenicians, Greeks or Romans, if not much earlier. Nobody really knows for certain. It is thought that, like lentils and chickpeas, they became part of eastern Mediterranean cuisine during the ne-olithic agricultural era, certainly by 6,000 BC (BCE).

Fava beans are apparently native to south-western Asia, from India to the Arabian peninsula and Asia Minor, and cul-tivation spread along Africa's Mediterranean coast — and then to Sicily — in the distant past. Fresh, chopped fava beans are one of the main ingredients of *falafels*. Favas are part of many Asian and African cuisines. In Egypt the spread known as *ful-medames*, consisting of mashed, boiled favas, olive oil, garlic and lemon juice has been very popular for centuries.

In Sicily the fava, harvested beginning in the middle of March, is used, along with fresh green wild artichokes and peas, to make *fritella*. Another popular dish is the soup known as *macco* or *maccu*, which can be made either with fresh (green) fava in springtime or from dried (tannish color) beans in au-tumn and winter. Macco contains little more than crushed fava beans and olive oil seasoned with a touch of onion, salt and pepper.

In fact, the natural flavor of the beans is so strong that recipes calling for fava rarely contain too many competing in-gredients. While fresh fava beans can be eaten raw, cooking brings out their distinctive flavor.

Creative recipes abound. Try mixing partially mashed, boiled fava into a *frittata* (omelet) made with Italian grated cheese. Boiled, crushed fava added to garlic sautéed in a good olive oil makes a great pasta condiment or a spread on crackers or bread.

Fava beans are full of natural fiber and they're a good source of many vitamins and minerals. This includes L-dopa, and in recent years fava beans have been recommended for those suffering from Parkinson's Disease.

The beans are high in tyramine. The food allergy associated with fava beans, appropriately called *favism,* occurs with some frequency in Mediterranean populations affected by anemic disorders (which evolved as a genetic response to malaria). Haemolytic anemia can result in those having this life-threatening allergy, and in some cases a reaction develops even if they merely inhale pollen from fava blossoms. More precisely, favism results from glucose-6-phosphate dehydrogenase (G6PD) deficiency, an X-linked recessive hereditary enzyme deficiency somewhat more frequent in children and men than in women. The condition is very rare and, in most cases, usually present without symptoms.

Fennel

At first glance a word like fennel seems pretty unambiguous. It's a plant with feathery yellowish-green foliage and yellow flowers that yields seeds with a distinctively spicy taste. Fennel is, in fact, often classified as a spice.

Would that it were quite so simple. To begin with, there are two Mediterranean plants often referred to as "fennel," and one happens to be what Italians often call *anise.* Then there's liquorice — actually an Asian plant bearing no near kinship to the fennels — which has a flavor similar to anise root. The Italian "liquorice liqueur" called *anisette* is, of course, made from local "anise root," not liquorice bean, and the idea that it contains elderberries is, well, just an idea.

True fennel is the plant known scientifically as *foeniculum vulgare,* and this is a case where the English and Italian words come directly from the Latin. Here in Sicily it's often called *finocchio di montagna* or "mountain fennel." This perennial, which actually grows wild in many areas, is in the *apiaceae* family (formerly *umbelliferae*). Indigenous to the Mediterranean, it thrives even in relatively dry climates. Mountain fennel rather resembles dill and in Sicilian cuisine it is usually served with pasta or as an ingredient in frittatas.

Then there's "Florentine" fennel. "Anise." This is *foeniculum vulgare azoricum,* distantly related to plain old *foeniculum vulgare.* Treated as an annual, this more "domesticated" fennel has a large white bulb (known by the misnomer "anise root") at its base near the roots. It is aromatic and, apart from its medicinal use, is a basic ingredient in absinthe. The bulb is edible and tastes a little like celery, containing high levels of various minerals, particularly iron, calcium, potassium and magnesium. It is also rich in Vitamin C and Vitamin B9 (folate). The anise bulb is popular in salads. It can be eaten raw but is sometimes grilled or baked.

Pedants will tell you that Florentine fennel is not true anise, but let's leave such complexities to the botanists. Suffice it to say that the same substance, *anethole,* which gives anise its flavor is present in Florentine fennel. Liquorice, unrelated to either anise and fennel, is *glycyrrhiza glabra,* a legume.

The Greek hero Prometheus made use of a fennel stalk to steal a flame from the gods. Perhaps that was the only kind of wood he could find. Mountain fennel has hollow stems and grows to a height of almost three metres (ten feet).

Fennel appears in the cuisines of the Middle East and Central Asia, including India, as well as China. Anethole is the medicinal component of fennel; its polymers act as phytoestrogens. And it tastes good enough that it is becoming known as something "exotic" outside countries where it is part of the traditional cuisine.

Figs

When Cato the Elder implored his fellow Romans to fight the Carthaginians, he showed the senators some fresh figs — supposedly from Carthage — to make them see just how close the African city was to Rome. Figs concealed the serpent whose venomous bite killed Cleopatra. The biblical Book of Kings defines peace and wealth as "each man under his own vine and fig tree." And, of course, fig leaves were what Adam and Eve used to conceal their nudity after having consumed the "forbidden fruit," which was most likely the product of a fig tree (not an apple tree as is commonly presumed). A chapter of the Koran is named for the fig tree, and Muhammed speaks of the fruit. In the *Lysistrata* of Aristophanes a young maiden wears a necklace made of dried figs as part of her initiation into womanhood.

Like almonds and olives, figs have an assured place in classical literature and the history of religion.

The common fig (ficus carica) is native to western Asia and the eastern Mediterranean and, like artichokes (thought to be indigenous to Sicily), probably grew wild in Sicily during the earliest times. It was domesticated long ago, in numerous cultivars and varieties, initially by the first neolithic farmers, and fossilized figs dated to circa 9400 BC (BCE) were discovered at one of the Gilgal village sites near Jericho.

Two varieties of fig are cultivated in Sicily. The "Italian White" is actually yellowish green, while the "Italian Black" ripens to a deep purple. They mature at about the same rate, and are ready to harvest beginning in late July.

Undomesticated wild figs also grow in Sicily. The green fruit, though edible, ripens in late August or early September and is small, and relatively bitter, with a thick skin. Like the nobler domesticated cultivars, this is a small tree.

While it is possible to propagate fig trees from seeds, shoots are the usual method. This means that, like most domesticated grape cultivars, domesticated fig trees are actually clones. Fig trees like water but can survive with little or no irrigation in coastal Mediterranean areas. Sunshine seems to sweeten the fruit, but a particularly dry summer may have a negative effect on production. Figs thrive in milder climates where the ground rarely freezes; some varieties are hardier than others.

Often dried, figs are a good source of fiber, potassium, calcium and other minerals, as well as antioxidants. *Buccellato,* a Sicilian winter specialty, is a crust stuffed with figs and nuts. Turkey and Egypt are the top producers of figs today. Sicily produces figs primarily for local consumption. A noble fruit, and an ancient one.

Hazelnuts

The humble hazelnut has grown across Europe for a very long time — at least since the Mesolithic period with one site dated to 7,000 BC (BCE) — making its way into northern regions like Ireland at the end of the last Ice Age and making its name as one of the oldest European foods. Hardy and nutritious, it seems ubiquitous. Here in Italy it is an ice cream flavor, *nocciola,* and a liqueur, *nocello,* and the base ingredient of hazelnut butter (Noce, as opposed to *nocciola,* is the walnut, also cultivated in Sicily.)

It is believed that the natural (indigenous) range of the hazelnut, genus *Corylus,* spans a broad area from north-western Europe across the northern Mediterranean and Balkans into Turkey, Persia and northern India.

Today, Turkey produces over seventy percent of the world's hazelnuts. In Sicily the hardy hazelnut is cultivated in the Madonie and Nebrodi mountains and around Etna, where the principal cultivars are of the *Tonda* varieties. It is harvested in late October, after the first chestnuts and olives, often by hand.

The Romans loved hazelnuts. Oddly, they are not a very important ingredient in Sicilian cuisine, nor are chestnuts. Not today, anyway. The predominance of almonds, which flourish in Sicily but don't grow in cooler climates, may explain this.

In some places hazelnuts, like chestnuts and acorns, are fed to livestock. That is not the case in Sicily, at least not since the Middle Ages. Compared to the almond, pine nut and walnut, hazelnuts are not generally considered a "noble" nut.

Also known as the cobnut, the hazelnut is the edible kernel of the cob of the hazel. This tasty seed has a thin, dark brown skin, which is edible.

Hazelnuts are high in healthy fats, protein, carbohydrates, various vitamins, folate, minerals (calcium, iron, magnesium, manganese, phosphorus, zinc and potassium) and dietary fiber.

Hazel trees are associated with truffles (see below).

Manna

"And when the dew that lay was gone up, behold, upon the face of the wilderness there lay a small round thing, as small as the hoar frost on the ground. And when the children of Israel saw it, they said one to another, It is manna: for they wist not what it was. And Moses said unto them, This is the bread which the Lord hath given you to eat. This is the thing which the Lord hath commanded, Gather of it every man according to his eating."

For most of us, the Book of Exodus is where we first heard about manna.

Literature is full of references to manna from Heaven, but what you find in Sicily is the real thing. Tasting vaguely like fresh maple sugar, *manna eletta* is a sweet product of the manna tree (fraxinus angustifolia), the narrow-leaf ash or manna ash, frassino in Italian. It contains only about three percent glucose by volume and is high in zinc. In Sicily this tree grows wild in the Madonie Mountains, and is now cultivated on farms in the area around Castelbuono and Pollina.

The whitish sap flows in July and August, forming thin stalactites which hang like icicles from the trees' branches. It is possible to harvest even more of it by splicing slits in the bark. The comparison to maple syrup is appropriate, though the composition of manna differs considerably from that popular American product. Manna is sold in small rods cut from the long drippings.

Much folklore has developed around manna, and also a great number of health claims, many of which are not scientifically substantiated. Yet the laxative value of the substance is well established, and as a natural sweetener (especially for diabetics and others who must watch their sugar intake) containing very little glucose manna is a heavenly gift.

We don't really know when the domesticated trees were introduced in Sicily. There are several obscure Greek references to manna trees. The Biblical descriptions are difficult to reconcile with the trees present in Sicily, whose name, however, certainly derives from the term used in the Book of Exodus.

The narrow-leaf ash, as distinguished from the closely-related European ash, has brown buds, and grows to a height of thirty meters. Its range is essentially central and western Mediterranean, though it is cultivated into central France. A subspecies (fraxinus oxycarpa) grows in eastern Europe as far north as the Czech Republic and in southwest Asia as far east as Iran. The wood of the manna ash is similar to that of other ashes.

Mushrooms

Mentioned in the previous chapter, these grow wild in the Nebrodi and Madonie Mountains.

Blood Oranges

It's difficult to know just when oranges were introduced into what is now Italy. From their travels to the southern and eastern reaches of their Empire, the Romans knew of them, and oranges are occasionally depicted in Roman art. However, it is generally accepted as fact that citrus fruits (oranges, lemons, citron) were first cultivated in Sicily during the Arab period. In other words, the ninth and tenth centuries. Indeed, the modern English word *orange,* like the Italian *arancia,* probably derives from the Arabic *naranj.* Oranges are native to tropical Asia, particularly the Malay region. Any reddish fruit in the genus citrus and the family rutaceae, specifically *citrus arantium,* is an orange.

Cultivation of oranges gradually spread through China and India to east Africa and then to the Mediterranean region. The trees prefer a mild climate, sunny weather and good drainage. An occasional frost or chill does not harm them. Originally, oranges had seeds.

Blood oranges are so called for their red flesh and deep red juice. When ripe, their skin may also be reddish, at least in part. In the British Empire, blood oranges were called "Maltese" oranges, and are closely related to Jaffa oranges. In Sicily, the most popular blood oranges are the *Tarocco,* the *Moro* and the *Sanguigno,* the latter cultivated extensively in the eastern part of the island as the *Sanguinello* of Paternò and Aderno. Though consumed in salads and desserts, blood oranges are favored for their distinctive red juice which, as it happens, is exceptionally healthy, being rich in antioxidants. Blood oranges are rarely very sweet.

Mandarins, Valencias and navel oranges are also grown in Sicily, but the blood orange is considered particularly Sicilian, perhaps because it is not as widely cultivated in Calabria, Spain or Greece.

Be warned that most of the orange drinks sold in Italy as being made from "Sicilian blood oranges," while they may contain some natural juice, are artificially colored.

Mulberries

Over the ages, kings and farmers alike favored mulberries; Charlemagne enjoyed the trees in his private garden, planted circa 812. Pliny, Ovid and Virgil wrote about the mulberry, which was raised on farms throughout the Italian peninsula. It was known by Greek chroniclers that the mulberry was a Persian fruit. Though the ancient Greeks or Phoenicians may have introduced the tree in Sicily, neither they nor the Romans undertook particularly widespread cultivation of the trees here. That distinction belongs to the Arabs.

The fruit, of course, was only a secondary reason for planting the mulberry trees in Sicily. The main purpose was the leaves of the hardy mulberry tree, favored by silkworms. During the Arab era and into the Norman period, Sicily became a center of silk production and silk weaving. Into the reign of Frederick II, royal robes were woven of Sicilian silk, and the fabric was exported across western Europe as far away as Scotland and Denmark. During the same period, the Moors popularized cultivation of the mulberry in their other major European dominion, Spain.

Morus nigra, the so-called "Black Persian Mulberry," the most common black mulberry, probably originated in China and has been cultivated in China, central Asia, India and Japan from a very early date. The tree is resilient, requiring less water than many other berry-producing plants. Not only are its berries delicious and therapeutic, and its leaves useful in silk making as well as animal feed, but the tree itself is a beautiful ornamental whose wood is artistically useful in carving. There is little doubt that it figured in the landscape of the extensive royal parks of Sicily's Norman and Swabian kings. Today, there are precious few mulberry trees in Sicily, and the prices of the fruit are expensive, but in the Middle Ages there were entire plantations of black and white mulberries, the latter preferred for silk production.

It is possible that Chinese silk production dates from around 3500 BC (BCE). In Egypt, silk was being made circa 1100 BC. Sericulture is almost a science in itself, but its techniques are universal. Spinning of silk fibers is still, for the most part, a traditional trade unaided by modern machinery.

The Sicilian silk industry is a thing of the past. Nowadays, most of Italy's silk comes from the communities around the northern city of Como, where the white mulberry is raised for this purpose.

Black mulberry trees, which are typically bushy and grow to a height of around ten meters (about thirty feet), have been known to live, and bear fruit, for centuries. (A living mulberry tree in Brentford, England, is believed to have been planted, from Persian stock, in 1548.) Botanically speaking, the sweet, juicy mulberry fruit is not actually a berry, but a collective fruit that grows to about 2.5 centimeters (about an inch) in length. A number of hybrids exist, but the three basic varieties were the American red mulberry (morus rubra), the white mulberry (morus alba) of China, and the black mulberry. Related species are the Korean mulberry (morus australis) and Himalayan mulberry (morus laevigata). *Moro* was the traditional Italian word for the mulberry tree; in modern Italian *gelso* is preferred.

Pistachios

Today, most of the pistachios consumed in Italy are imported from Iran and Iraq. That wasn't always the case. Throughout the Middle Ages, the pistachios consumed by Sicilians came from eastern Sicily, where they are still grown, particularly around Mount Etna and in the Bronte area. There are a few other localities known for their pistachios, and here Raffadali comes to mind. Traditionally cultivated in India, central Asia, the Middle East and the eastern Mediterranean, pistachios were introduced in Sicily in ancient times, probably by the Phoenicians, the Sicels or the earliest Greek colonizers.

There is little doubt that the ninth-century Arab rulers of Sicily encouraged the wider cultivation of the tasty nuts. It was probably the Arabs who began the practice of radically pruning pistachio trees every two years to increase nut production. Pistachios found their way into many of the sweet confections still made today, created in Fatimid Sicily using cane sugar. That's how most of Sicily's pistachio production is now used — either in pastries or in ice cream.

Sicilian pistachios are slightly longer and thinner than those grown in the Middle East. They also seem to have a stronger, sharper taste, due perhaps in part to the volcanic soil in which they're grown. They are not exported in large quantities. Unlike olive growers, pistachio farmers receive little economic support from the Italian government. Here in Sicily, almonds seem to have been preferred to pistachios, probably because the cultivation of pistachios was historically more difficult. Almond trees, which require somewhat less water, seem generally hardier than pistachio plants.

Pistacia Vera is the edible variety of pistachio grown in warm, dry climates around the world, even in California. The pistachio tree is an evergreen native to Asia, and the very word traces the fruit's origin. The English word *pistachio* comes to us from the Old Italian *pistaccio,* from the Greek *pistakion*, which in turn derives from an Old Persian word. The Sicilian *fatuk* and *fastuka* is of Arabic origin.

Pistachios are a good source of protein, fat, fiber, vitamin B6 and thiamine. The mature kernels are generally greenish with reddish areas, assuming a brownish color when toasted.

However, it is possible to eat them dried rather than toasted.

Widely regarded as a snack food, pistachios are well-suited to Italian recipes, including some that call for pine nuts. Pistachios are excellent in rice dishes or as a garnish in main courses.

Squash

Several varieties of *zucchini* are popular in Sicily. These are American species brought to Sicily by the Spaniards.

Cocuzza, or *cucuzza,* is a long, green "squash" sometimes called *zucchina.* Strictly speaking, it is a gourd.

Tinniruma, sometimes *tenerumi,* are the green tips and leaves of cocuzza or Italian zucchini. The word *tenerumi* causes confusion because it is widely misused.

Zuccata, also *cucuzzata,* are sugared squash preserves.

Several *cucurbita* varieties have been cultivated in Sicily for centuries. This includes the classic Hubbard squashes and a type similar to pumpkin.

Truffles

The hazels and oaks of the Nebrodi Mountains provide the perfect growth environment for truffles, traditionally detected with the aid of Nebrodian black pigs. The rare wild Sicilian truffles are related to *Tuber borchii* found in the southern regions of peninsular Italy. These are light in color. What is sometimes cultivated is *Tuber brumale,* which has a dark color.

Watermelon

Gelo di melone, a sweet gelatine dessert made from watermelon pulp, has been made in Sicily every summer for centuries. It is thought to be Arab in origin, but this is uncertain.

What is certain is that watermelons have been raised in Sicily since the Middle Ages, and that, like so many other crops, they were introduced by the Arabs.

In antiquity watermelons were cultivated in the Nile Valley. However, although watermelon seeds have been found in the tombs of Egyptian pharaohs and at archeological sites in Ethiopia and around the Middle East, the delicious fruit, native to southern Africa, does not appear to have been very widely cultivated north of the Sahara until medieval times.

There is some controversy in these matters: Did the ancient Romans know of such crops? Were citrus fruits (for example) cultivated in some parts of their vast Empire? It's really a question of permanency and diffusion. The point is that the continuous cultivation of certain fruits, including watermelons, is identified in the Mediterranean with the centuries following the fall of the Roman Empire.

Citrullus Lanatus, which Italians call *anguria,* is today one of the most common varieties of melon (itself a loose term as most melons are in the genus Cucumis). By the eleventh century the sweet red flesh in a green rind was popular in Sicily and as far away as eastern Asia, where some Japanese farmers grow them in square containers, thus developing a square fruit.

Watermelons, which are more than ninety percent water, are a good source of ascorbic acid (Vitamin C), beta carotene, lycopene and potassium. The flesh of some varieties is orange or yellow, and in recent times watermelons of other colors have been bred.

Except in Asia, there is surprisingly little legend and folklore surrounding the watermelon. Admittedly, not much can be said about a fruit which is, at best, a complement to other foods. July and August see a great quantity of watermelons sold at stands around Sicily. Not only gelo di melone, but granita and sorbets are flavored with watermelon, which seems the quintessential warm-weather fruit.

CHAPTER 5

Appetizers, Side Dishes, Salads

"First came a spice-laden haze, then chicken livers, hard boiled eggs, sliced ham, chicken and truffles in masses of piping hot, glistening macaroni, to which the meat juice gave an exquisite hue of suede."

— Giuseppe Tomasi di Lampedusa, *The Leopard*

Except at the most formal dinners, many rules seem to have gone the way of the Kingdom of Sicily — something revealed only in traces of tradition. Yet, as we've already mentioned, Sicilian meals do have something of a structure, perhaps even a faint ethos.

The *antipasto* is a starter, an appetizer. The *contorno* is a side dish served with the *secondo,* the main course, following the *primo,* which is usually pasta. Salads might be served at the beginning or end of a meal, or as a snack.

What we now call "street food" used to be appetizers for the rich or simple meals for the poor.

Categories may overlap, but there's a method to the madness.

To your authors falls the task of exposing a few appealing "Italian" things as not-quite-Italian. Perhaps, like us, you have encountered these in places like New York and London, where a creative restaurateur described them as "Sicilian." In those delightful, cosmopolitan cities one now finds restaurants that serve, as an appetizer, bread for dipping in olive oil, with patrons invited to soak up the greenish liquid using the bread as if it were a sponge. A more American invention is "garlic bread." Then there's the "Sicilian" pizza that resembles nothing you'll find here in Sicily.

Here in Italy, the only time you are likely to be served white bread with olive oil is at a formal olive oil tasting, usually between sips of each oil. Italians serve bread with meals, but we don't consider it an appetizer in itself unless, perhaps, it is a very specific recipe like olive bread — a loaf with olives mixed into it — or bruschetta. Bread might accompany a platter of hams and cheeses, a *tagliere*.

The simple fact is that almost *anything* can be served as an antipasto, a side dish or an offering at a buffet. At best, we can provide a very general idea of what is most traditional. These typical dishes are described in the following pages, a few in the recipe chapter. Here's a short list.

Arancini: Stuffed rice balls. What you are most likely to be served as an appetizer are mini arancini.

Aubergine Salad: This is *caponata,* or eggplant salad, made with aubergines, olives and capers.

Beccafico: Fresh roasted herring (sardines) rolled and stuffed with a mixture of traditional ingredients.

Bruschetta: Toasted bread topped with chilled chopped tomatoes, onions, olives and herbs.

Cheeses: As appetizers, these are usually aged, served with hams. A popular Palermitan recipe is *cacio all'argentiera* (fried caciocavallo).

Crocchè: Fried potato and cheese dumplings, croquettes, sometimes called *cazzilli*.

Fritedda: Cooked, fresh green fava beans, peas, and artichoke hearts. Also *fritella*.

Hams and Salame: The most traditional Sicilian prosciutto is made from the Nebrodian black swine.

Maccu: Creamy winter soup made from dried fava beans and fennel. Also *macco*.

Olives: As an appetizer, these are either cured or (especially for black olives) baked.

Orange Salad: There are several variations here, some featuring bits of anchovy or sardine.

Panella: Flat fried cakes made with ceci bean flour.

Pastella: The phrase in pastella refers to anything battered and fried, typically cardoons, broccoli and artichoke hearts.

Tagliere: Literally a wooden cutting board, this is a means of serving cheeses and hams, as opposed to a china platter.

Tomatoes: As an appetizer, usually stuffed.

Vegetables: These might be *giri* (chards), wild asparagus, artichokes or anything that is in season.

CHAPTER 6

Street Food

"Palermo, where we stayed eight days, was lovely. The most beautifully situated town in the world, it dreams away its life in the Conca d'Oro, the exquisite valley that lies between two seas. The lemon groves and the orange gardens were so entirely perfect."

— Oscar Wilde, *Letters*

Palermo and Catania are full of stands and street vendors selling what has come to be called *street food*. Some of these specialties are also offered in restaurants, usually as the kind of *antipasti* (appetizers) that Sicilians sometimes call *stuzzichini*. These used to be called "finger foods" because, like hamburgers, they could be consumed without the aid of a fork.

Most of these are described in greater detail elsewhere in

this volume. Let's consider this brief summary a fast, simple introduction.

Arancini. These are fried rice balls filled with meat. One is depicted on the cover of this book. Although there are giant and mini arancini, the normal size is slightly over 5 centimeters (2 inches) in diameter. Nowadays, they are made with all manner of fillings, from salmon to spinach to chicken. If we had to judge quality, we would say that the sensation of a crunchy "skin" on the first bite is a good initial sign.

Chestnuts. During the Winter these are sold roasted by street vendors.

Crispella. This is a fritter stuffed with either ricotta and anchovies (salty version), or coated with honey (sweet version).

Crocchè. These are *croquettes,* fried potato and cheese dumplings, and in this book we present a good traditional recipe. Our criticism is that what you buy from street vendors usually lacks much cheese and mint.

Frittola. This consists of small pieces of fried beef offal. It is not as popular now as it was in the past.

Gelato. Ice cream cones and ice cream sandwiches. Arguably street food, these are often sold in tiny *gelaterie.*

Pastella. This describes anything deep-fried in a thick batter, especially broccoli, carduna or artichoke hearts, sometimes chunks of eggplant. Sardines are also battered (lightly) and sold this way.

Panella. This is a thin, flat, fried "cake," usually about 8 centimeters (3 inches) square, made with ceci bean flour, often served as an appetizer.

Scacciata. A focaccia filled with meat and vegetables, popular in Catania.

Semenza. A mix of seeds and shelled nuts, most popular at festivals. This might include pumpkin seeds, small toasted ceci and other things.

Sfincione. This is a thick Sicilian pizza topped with tomatoes, onions and anchovies. It is rarely served in pizzerias but available in focaccerias, some bakeries, or from street vendors. (To Sicilians, this is not considered *pizza,* which in Italy is by definition thin and crusty.) The local variation in Trapani is *rianata.* A street vendor of sfincione is a *sfincionaro.*

Spleen Sandwiches. *Pane con la milza,* sometimes made with beef lung instead of beef spleen, which is traditional. Cooked in lard, the spleen may be topped with grated cheese or flavored with lemon juice. The vendor is a *vastiddaru,* for the *vastedda* bread traditionally used in preparing these sandwiches.

Stigghiola. Fried or roasted calf or ovine intestines, similar to American chitlins.

CHAPTER 7

Grains, Pasta, Bread, Pizza

"Trabia lies at a charming site, full of streams and mills on a beautiful plain where vermicelli is made on large farms and exported to Calabria as well as other Muslim and Christian lands."

— Idrisi, *The Book of King Roger*

Nobody knows exactly when grain was domesticated in Sicily, but a theory tied to the "Neolithic Revolution" and some temples in Turkey erected over ten thousand years ago, complemented by sophisticated genetic studies, suggests that it was quite early. Not that any of these scholarly matters need concern us very excessively here. It's enough to say that wheat and bread have been known in Sicily since antiquity, and that the results are enticing.

Rice, along with certain kinds of wheat, was introduced by the Arabs in the ninth or tenth century. Sophisticated canal systems nourished the rice, and the wheat was a variety that could flourish with very little water. So much for the history of graniculture.

By 1500, Sicily relied too heavily on wheat, so famines resulted from bad harvests. Italy has been importing wheat for centuries. Domestic production would be insufficient for the pasta the country makes and exports. Indeed, it would be insufficient to feed sixty million Italians. Nevertheless, it remains a dietary staple.

Whole, unmilled wheat grain finds its way into cuccìa, described in our dessert chapter.

Until just a few years ago, it was all but impossible to find grain products in Sicily suitable for those suffering from celiac disease. That is no longer the case, but rather few restaurants and pizzerias offer gluten-free food.

Bread

Traditional Sicilian bread is either "white" or, if made with the durum wheat flour used to make pasta, "macinato." There was never much barley, rye or pumpernickel in Sicily.

But that's not to suggest that Sicilian bakers are lacking in creative impulses. There is, for example, "votive" bread sculpture — bread formed into complex shapes like the faces of saints for religious feasts. In Agrigento and Mussomeli there's San Calogero bread, formed into a leg or head or whichever part of the body was cured in response to prayer. San Biagio Platani has an annual bread festival featuring giant arches made of bread.

Whole wheat is a recent introduction. Here the traditional Sicilian entry is *tumminia,* made with a flour ground from the whole grain of durum wheat, including the germ. This is Sicilian *pane nero,* "black bread," which is dense in consistency but not very black.

A popular soft bread used in sandwiches is *vastedda,* which shares the name of a cheese.

There are several types of seasoned or filled bread. Olive bread comes to mind, but there is also *focaccia,* a crusty bread flavored with spices and herbs, and *scacciata,* a focaccia filled with meat and vegetables, popular in Catania. *Muffuletta* is a bread sometimes made with anchovies.

Pasta

Pasta needs no grandiose introduction. It is ubiquitous around the world.

As we've mentioned, spaghetti, or something very much like it, was being made in Trabia in the twelfth century, and during the next century Frederick II was being served something like lasagne. Without wishing to complicate matters, we suggest that there are essentially two kinds of pasta.

"Fresh" pasta consists of *tortellini,* which are stuffed with meat, cheese or vegetables and formed into tiny wreaths with the fingers, and *ravioli,* which are usually larger than tortellini, being cut into defined shapes. Tortellini is the more classically Sicilian of the two.

Macaroni covers just about every other type of pasta. This may be freshly-made rather than dried, and comes in too many shapes to be listed here. It is usually made in moulds or pushed through dies to achieve its distinctive shapes.

Generically referred to in our times as *pasta,* macaroni forms go by different names around Italy. In Sicily two of the most popular are *anelletti,* the "rings" used in baked pasta, and *bucatini,* the tubular strands used in pasta with fennel and sardines.

Yes, we know that some chefs and food writers refer only

to pasta that is tubular as "macaroni." They are the same people who only call hard, crunchy Italian cookies *biscotti* (see the pastry chapter). Before the twentieth century *most* dried pasta sold commercially was called *macaroni* by Italians. In Palermo there is even a street called *Via dei Maccheronai,* literally the "street of the macaroni makers."

Polenta

Made from cornmeal, this is a northern Italian specialty that was never very popular in Sicily. It seems to have made its first significant appearance here with our island's brief rule by the House of Savoy in the early years of the eighteenth century. Nobody seemed to like it any more than they liked nasty King Vittorio Amedeo of Savoy. The maize (corn) grown in Sicily is not usually one of the tender hybrids developed in the United States but a tougher variety similar to what Americans call "cow corn" because it is fed to cattle.

Rice

This is no longer raised in Sicily, where there are few traditional rice recipes except the rice ball, or *arancina,* which we have already met. There are now Sicilian *risotto* recipes, such as risotto with artichokes, but these are something of a novelty. Here we'd just like to say that Canaroli and Arborio are the only rices that should be used in preparing risotto, though there is more latitude in arancini.

Couscous

This is a granular food made from *semola* of durum wheat, similar to pasta. It may even be considered an early form of pasta, but while pasta is made from flour — produced from finely ground grains of durum wheat — semola actually comes from the coarse pieces remaining after most of the grain has been ground. Couscous should not be confused with *tabouleh,* a cold salad made with the coarser, crunchier bulgur, also derived from a variety of wheat, though in Sicily a kind of pseudo-taboule made with couscous-type semola is served in restaurants. Semola is much finer, softer, pastier and stickier than bulgur, resembling and tasting more like pasta than like chips of grain.

Culinary historians used to believe that couscous, which is popular in Tunisia and other parts of northern Africa, was reintroduced in Sicily after 1600 following an absence of four centuries, but it seems to have been prepared in the Trapani, Sciacca and Marsala areas continuously since Arab times. There's an old Sicilian word for it, cuscusu, which may be traced to the fourteenth century. The earliest form of couscous was probably made with millet.

Among the numerous couscous recipes, each region has its own variations, with Sicily's being less spicy than Tunisia's or Libya's.

Based on what appears to be a fairly modern recipe (including ingredients discovered in the Americas after 1500), Sicilian couscous is made of rapidly steamed, flavored semola (prepared with fish or meat broth) "dried" and topped with either a fish or meat based sauce of vegetables, usually including potatoes, carrots, onions, celery, parsley, garlic, a few peeled tomatoes, olive oil, paprika, saffron and other spices.

A specific method and utensils are used in the process, and the couscous and sauce are served in separate terra cotta bowls, diners serving themselves as much of the sauce as they wish. Meat couscous usually contains chunks of beef and either lamb (or mutton), goat meat or rabbit.

Classic *couscous alla trapanese* is the fish-and-seafood couscous for which Trapani is famous. It contains a deep-sea "white" fish such as snapper or sea bass (or cod) with the addition of mussels or shrimp. There is no single recipe for it but literally dozens. This is really a cool-weather dish. A visit to Erice or nearby Trapani is hardly complete without a bowl of couscous. In nearby San Vito lo Capo there's an annual couscous festival in late September.

Sfincione

This is a thick Sicilian pizza topped with tomatoes, onions, a few anchovies and perhaps grated caciocavallo cheese, seasoned with a dash of oregano. Outside Italy, the term "Sicilian pizza" is used to describe all kinds of things, but until the 1860s sfincione was the kind of "pizza" usually consumed in Sicily, especially in the western part of the island.

With a spongy crust up to two centimetres (an inch) thick, sfincione is more like bread than pizza, which in Italy usually has a thin crust. Culinary writers like to wax poetic about its origins. In fact, sfincione as we know it today has been made only since the seventeenth century. The most important ingredient, the tomato, is South American in origin.

The tomatoes are essential, but the real flavor of sfincione comes from the onions, sautéed in olive oil before baking.

Focaccia is a crusty bread flavored with spices and herbs. *Bruschetta* are slices of toasted bread seasoned with chopped tomatoes, olive oil and other toppings.

There's a recipe in our recipe chapter.

Pizza

Pizza, as we know it today, is essentially a Neapolitan invention that evolved from these other specialities. In Naples the most popular recipe was the *margherita,* named for a queen of Italy, made with tomatoes, mozzarella and fresh basil leaves, thus representing the colors of Italy (red, white and green).

In addition to a base of tomato sauce and a layer of mozzarella, toppings — which Italians call *condimenti* — abound: hams (prosciutto, speck), salami, sausage, bresaola, guanciale, mushrooms, peppers, onions, aubergines, olives, tomato chunks, cheeses (gorgonzola, provolone) and artichokes. Even slices of anchovy or smoked salmon find their way onto pizza. Fresh leaves of basil and arugula are also popular.

Pizza is Sicily's most popular take-out and restaurant food. Chicken on a skewer remains popular as take-away, but only a distant second to pizza.

Varieties abound, but the quintessential Sicilian pizza is the *capricciosa*. This usually includes tomato sauce, mozzarella, mushrooms, onions, ham, artichokes, olives and perhaps a few chunks of eggplant. A wurstel is usually placed atop these toppings.

In Sicily the pizza served in a pizzeria is large and circular, about 28 centimeters (11 inches) in diameter, really a meal in itself. The pizza *a taglio* sold by bakeries is baked in square pans and, frankly, cannot hold a candle to what you'll get in a good pizzeria that uses an old-fashioned wood oven with an open flame.

CHAPTER 8

Fish and Seafood

"A man of such stature indulging in almost obscene metaphors, displaying an infantile appetite for the altogether mediocre pleasure of eating sea urchins!"

— Giuseppe Tomasi di Lampedusa, *The Professor and the Mermaid*

Here in Sicily, much of the same fish and seafood have been served the same way for centuries. That may change as some species are "hunted" to extinction. The fishing tradition that most resembles hunting involves large tuna.

The Mattanza

For hundreds of years, fishermen in Sicily and Sardinia have used dense nets to capture the Mediterranean *bluefin tuna* (thunnus thinnus) in a quasi-spiritual procedure known as the *mattanza*. This takes place in May and June, when the giant fish swim past the coasts. In Sicily, the few remaining mattanzas take place off the island's western point among the coastal Egadi Islands. The term *mattanza* comes to us from an old Spanish word, *matar,* meaning "to kill." Many terms, such as *rais* (head fisherman of the mattanza), are actually Arabic in origin. There are indications that the mattanza, in some form, originated in the Phoenician or Carthaginian era. Averaging over two hundred kilograms (over four hundred pounds), the fish are now popular in the Japanese market, where the delicious red meat is used in sashimi and sushi. It must be said that this fresh tasty meat is a breed apart from the bland whitish stuff sold in cans. Bluefin, many of which escape into the Atlantic, may also be consumed young.

The keys to a successful mattanza, apart from the obvious questions of supply (overfishing has reduced the number of larger tuna in recent years) and weather, are organisation and technique. A series of vast nets are lowered into the water. The tuna are captured in successive nets which are gradually restricted in size and raised toward the surface, where the fish are attacked with what might be described as large spears in a sophisticated trap system.

Reaching 4.3 meters (14 feet) in length and weighing as much as 800 kilograms (1800 pounds), the bluefin is the largest tuna, surpassing the skipjack, albacore, yellowfin and bigeye. Unlike these other worldwide species, the bluefin lives in the Atlantic and Mediterranean.

The network of net chambers is called an *isola* (island). One of the interesting things about the mattanza is the team effort of the numerous fishermen involved in each catch. From his boat, the rais directs the work of the men in the other small boats. Because a mattanza is the catch of an entire school of fish, dozens of tuna may be captured. The ambience of bloody water and particularly large fish, which might be compared to cattle or large game, leaves one with a singular impression. There's nothing like watching the fish struggle as they are herded into ever smaller, shallower net chambers — the final one is called the "chamber of death" — and finally lifted onto the boats. Indeed, the term *mattanza* has found its way into the Italian vernacular as a synonym for "massacre."

Just how long the mattanza itself survives remains to be seen. As time passes, the tuna are diminishing in size and numbers, while demand increases in world markets. This has prompted legal restrictions. A hundred years ago, there were dozens of small *tonnare* (tuna canneries) along the Sicilian coasts, though in Sicily the word *tonnara* originally referred to the complex series of nets used in tuna fishing during the mattanza. The occupation of tuna fishing was more widespread, with hundreds of *tonnarotti* (tuna fishermen) throughout Sicily. Tunny fishing has usually been a seasonal profession in Sicily, with the tonnarotti catching other fish during the autumn and winter.

Breaded fried tuna steaks are a traditional Sicilian specialty. Tuna steaks are also tasty simply grilled with onions and served with fresh mint.

Bottarga, mentioned in an earlier chapter, is dried tuna roe sometimes sprinkled over pasta.

Cuttlefish

There must be an entire category of "exotic" foods, made from unusual plants and animals, that most people have never heard of. One of those frequently overlooked is *seppia,* or cuttlefish.

Some cuttlefish prosper in certain regions, such as the Mediterranean, while avoiding others like the northern Atlantic. They prefer warmer waters.

To most of us, this squid-like creature is best known for its boney internal shell, the cuttlebone. Rich in calcium and chalky

111

in texture when dry, the cuttlebone is placed in the cages of birds like parrots so that our winged friends can grind their beaks on it. For those of us without feathers, there are two edible parts of the seppia — the flesh which tastes like octopus or squid, and the dark ink. The ink, incidentally, is the natural coloring used in making black pasta, and it's more viscous than squid ink. Tastier, too, according to connoisseurs.

Seppia ink is also a main ingredient of a popular pasta sauce but first we should mention its historical use in the actual ink used for writing. The word *sepia* refers to a dark brown color associated with old photographs. In fact, the term is rooted in references to the faded tone of writing inks made from cuttlefish ink, which remains distinct for centuries.

By definition, cuttlefish belong to the order *sepiida* and are of course distantly related to squids, but the largest cuttlefish do not reach the dimensions of their cousins. The cuttlebone provides buoyancy to the creature, which can alter its color somewhat (a few octopi can do this) and has exceptionally good vision.

Despite its black color, seppia sauce, or *nero di seppia,* is only part ink. It also contains seppia chunks, olive oil, sautéed garlic or onions, tomato puree (or paste), white wine, parsley and pepper. The ink is easily extracted from the glands of the cooked cuttlefish. The sauce is best with long pasta like linguine. Remember that in Italy fish and seafood are never accompanied by grated cheese.

Sea Urchins

The English word *urchin* originally referred to the hedgehog, and the Sicilian (and Medieval Italian) *riccio* still does. In former times the sea urchin's "spines" were compared to those of the creature that resembles a porcupine. Since hardly anybody eats hedgehog anymore (it's a protected species still seen in Sicily), it seems fairly obvious that *ricci* served with pasta are sea urchins, which have been consumed in the Mediterranean region from the most ancient times.

Sea urchins are rather small, spiny, creatures having a hard, globular shell, the *test* (from the Latin, French and Italian words for "head"), which is usually less than ten centimetres in diameter. They live in all the world's oceans and in the Mediterranean. While urchins vary in size and color, those in the Med are usually a dark, purplish hue, almost black, with the test averaging just over six centimetres (almost three inches) in diameter and the spines adding another few centimetres. With sand dollars, they make up the class *echinoidea* in the *echinoderm* phylum. More broadly, the phylum also includes crinoids, star fish and sea cucumbers. *Echinodermate* literally means "spiny skin" in Classical Greek.

Urchins use their spines, which are actually "feet," to move very slowly, usually on the sea floor but often in relatively shallow waters, feeding on algae. Eels and certain other adventurous sea life, such as the occasional octopus, eat urchins. Fearing the sharp spines, many fish avoid them. Some fish are smarter than they look.

Regarded as something of a delicacy today, urchins are eaten raw and feature in the cuisines of most Mediterranean cultures. Efforts have been made to discourage over-harvesting. Unlike mussels, urchins are rarely raised on farms, though this may change as they become scarcer in the wild.

The mouth of the urchin is in its lower half, and the shell is actually divided into five parts. None of this is very obvious to the untrained eye. It is thought that the spines of some urchins are poisonous, but those in the central Mediterranean are just painful when they get stuck in your hand. Heavy gloves are essential equipment in harvesting and cracking open (with a hammer or heavy meat cleaver) fresh urchins.

And fresh is the only way they should be eaten. It may seem like a culinary cliché, but canned urchins have no flavor. The point is that fresh urchins don't have a "fishy" odor or taste.

Like truffles, which have a unique taste, their flavor is difficult to describe because no other seafood tastes quite like urchins. Their flavor is vaguely similar to that of fresh mussels, but the comparison is a tenuous one. This just isn't the same thing as observing that, for example, cuttlefish, octopus and squid all have a similar taste.

Sicilian diners often use soft white bread to scoop out the meaty center of the urchin while trying to avoid any piece of shell or spine remaining from the chopping process and ending up inside. Obviously, it's ideal to harvest urchins in clear, clean water. Unfortunately, Sicily's coastal waters aren't as clean as they used to be, a factor that has reduced the level of edible algae — and with it the urchin population — in recent years. Then there's the problem of overzealous (and illegal) harvesting.

Urchins are considered a cool-weather food. In Sicily you usually begin to find them sold in the middle of November, and by late April the urchin season is over.

There are various recipes for urchin sauce. Most include sautéed garlic or onion (never both), the pulp of some fresh, chopped, skinned tomatoes (but not too much as this is not a tomato sauce), a touch of fresh parsley or mint (maybe even a dash of both), salt, freshly-ground pepper and extra-virgin (and unfiltered) olive oil. Perhaps a little butter. A guiding principle is that nothing should overpower the flavor of the urchin meat. The pasta should be vermicelli, spaghetti or (ideally) thin linguine of the best quality available.

Herring and Sardines

The herring in Sicily are large sardines. By definition, the sardine is any small herring rather than a particular species of fish. Even if you don't like the canned variety, you may enjoy the fresh ones. A popular recipe is *beccafico,* sardines rolled and stuffed; in Agrigento they're served flat. *Pasta con sarde* is a pasta sauce of sardines and fennel. *Neonata* (literally "newborn") is a mass of quasi-transparent baby sardines (a few days old) served as a sauce or fried; it is now illegal to harvest and sell these. A sardine that is an inch long is not "neonata" but probably two or three weeks old when caught and cooked.

Swordfish

Swordfish is sold in thin circular slices, or "steaks," which might be roasted or broiled, served with olive oil, lemon and a touch of mint. Other popular recipes are *involtini* (stuffed rolls) and *pasta alla barcaiola,* a sauce made with chunks of fish and aubergines. Sailfish also makes an occasional appearance in Sicilian street markets.

Snapper, Mullet, Grouper

A popular recipe is *cipollata* or *stemperata,* the fish prepared in a glaze of onions, vinegar and sugar.

Mackerel

This fish has a strong flavor. Smaller, plate-size mackerels are often grilled over a fire, but they may also be baked in an oven. The smallest ones, *sgombretti,* may be cleaned (but not boned), dredged in flour and fried, which is a common recipe for fresh sardines.

Mussels

These are usually raised on farms such as those along Sicily's northeastern coast near Milazzo and the Aeolian Islands. A popular recipe is mussels and a lightly-cooked sauce of fresh tomatoes, but they are often served steamed with a halved lemon.

Squid and Octopus

Calamari are served grilled (whole) or fried (sliced into rings). A classic Sicilian recipe for stuffed squid is included in our recipe chapter. That is a recipe favored by the aristocracy. Be warned that the "stuffed" squid served in folksier Sicilian restaurants may contain little more than loose, dried bread crumbs with a few pine nuts and raisins mixed into these. Closely related is the octopus, sometimes roasted but usually boiled.

Scabbard Fish

Spatola has white flesh and a very delicate texture. What is usually served is a fillet about as long as the diameter of a plate. Sometimes it is rolled and stuffed, very much like beccafico (for herring).

Dolphin Fish

This is what Sicilians call *capone*, literally "big head." It is believed to have been an ingredient in caponata (aubergine salad) in times past.

Anchovies

In Sicily these are either fresh or salted, used as an accent in various recipes. Fresh anchovies are sometimes served marinated in lemon juice.

Shrimp

Gamberoni are "jumbo shrimp" or prawns. Color ranges from pinkish to deep red. In Italy red prawns are the most prized. These are usually grilled or roasted whole. The smaller shrimp served in rice and pasta are *gamberetti*.

Clams, Scallops, Oysters

These are rather rare in Sicilian waters. What is served in restaurants is usually purchased frozen from suppliers of Atlantic seafood. The fresh clams one finds in Sicilian street markets are invariably small.

Eels

Until the 1950s there were still freshwater eels to be found in a few Sicilian streams. What is sold at the street markets in Catania and Palermo are various types of sea eel. Restaurants serve this only rarely.

Shark

Palombo, sometimes *palumbo,* is smooth-hound, or hound shark, a small, edible shark that Americans sometimes call "dog fish." Usually served fresh, these are an interesting sight at street market stands where, reposing on a bed of crushed ice, they seem almost alive and quite dangerous.

Snails

We're talking about ground snails that like moisture but have never been near a beach, let alone a large body of water. (Sorry, we just didn't know where else to include the delightful creatures.)

Harvested in the wild beginning in the Spring, snails make their most prominent culinary appearance during the Summer for the Feast of Saint Rosalie, Palermo's patron saint. The Sicilian name for the tiny but tasty snails is *babbaluci,* a word that comes to us from the Arabic. In Maltese, actually Siculo-Arabic, the word is *bebbux.*

It should be mentioned that the most popular snail in Sicilian cuisine is a small variety of *Helix aspersa,* the European brown snail, found in the greener areas of the European Mediterranean and North Africa. This is what is usually referred to as *babbaluci.* The larger *Helix Aspersa Maxima* snails are called *crastuni.*

A rarer species identified scientifically only in 1832 is its slightly larger, distant cousin, *Cornu mazzullii,* which thrives in north-western Sicily between Trapani and Cefalù. The *Cornu* is endangered and therefore not harvested, officially at least. *Muccuni,* incidentally, are "sea snails."

Outside kitchens, *Cornu* is what is usually meant by the generic term "Sicily snail." The much larger French *escargot* is *Helix pomatia.*

It is possible that ground snails became a popular food during Sicily's Arab period, but they were certainly consumed here long before the ninth century. Ground snail farming, called *heliciculture,* is a much more recent development. Most snails consumed in Sicily nowadays are farmed.

Oddly enough, babbaluci are not usually served with pasta. More often, they are boiled in salt water, following a day soaking in cold water or perhaps a container of flour. They are served with a condiment made of finely-diced celery stalk, parsley and garlic, and lightly sautéed in olive oil seasoned with salt and pepper. But the diminutive Sicilian snails are not removed from their tiny shells as easily as the French escargots. Instead, toothpicks are used.

Recipes for babbaluci abound and, yes, there are a few recipes for babbaluci with pasta. This is one of those cases when only a local ingredient will suffice. It's not easy to find Sicilian-type snails outside the central Mediterranean, though smaller French ones may suffice in a pinch. Enjoy them with a Sicilian white wine.

CHAPTER 9

Meats

"They find their way to the magnificent court of Hieron, who brandishes the scepter of dooms in Sicily, rich in flocks, reaping the crested heads of every excellence."

— Pindar, *The Odes*

Meat. Only in Sicily could a simple definition be so complicated. For the sake of conversation, let's say that meat is anything that begins its life on four legs. Well, almost anything.

Why the complexity? Our vegetarian friends tell us that poultry and fish are, according to certain definitions, meat. We agree, of course, that these are all living creatures, but for our purposes let's focus on the Sicilian context, which is already confusing enough.

Some historians like to point out that until the 1960s many

Sicilian families consumed meat only once or twice each week. That's half true because chicken and fish, which many people did eat more frequently than beef, pork or lamb, were not regarded as "meat" by statisticians or by the majority of Sicilians themselves.

Hardly anybody in Sicily consumes horse meat anymore, but until a few years ago Palermo had at least a dozen butchers who sold it. A few of these shops were actually dedicated to *carne equina*. We remember one in the Vucciria street market where there were numerous horse figurines lined up in a row in a kind of collection, perhaps to remind less literate customers of what was sold there. Horse meat butcher shops seem to have survived in greater numbers in Catania than in Palermo.

Decades ago, there were even people who did not consider sausage to be meat. And then there's offal. Is tripe meat? What about goat brain?

To this day, chicken is rarely served in restaurants in southern Italy. Poultry was historically something people raised and prepared at home. In the cities, however, you'll find *pollerie* that serve chicken roasted over a flame on a skewer. This situation isn't too different from what once existed in the United States, where in times past southern fried chicken was something found more often in homes than in restaurants, with recipes guarded as coveted family secrets.

Rabbit and hare, formerly more popular in Sicily, were not always considered meat. Some people raised rabbits and pigeons with every intention of eating them. In Italy you still find fresh rabbit sold in supermarkets. Rabbit is usually found in the poultry section, but the day we see a rabbit with wings will be the day pigs can fly.

Speaking of pigs, most of the pork consumed in Sicily is imported from the Netherlands, France and Germany. Most of the beef is also imported, though some of it is Italian.

Yet Sicily is one of the few places where you can still purchase fresh meat from a butcher who cuts and chops it while you wait. There's something to be said for that.

Pork

The indigenous variety is the Nebrodian black swine, its name protected by Italian and European norms, and some *prosciutto* (ham) is made from it. However, too few of these hardy, boarish hogs are raised in Sicily to supply even a fraction of the demand for pork. Much of the ham and bacon sold in Sicily comes from Parma or elsewhere in northern Italy.

Breaded pork cutlets are a Sicilian regional specialty. Another is sausage *alla pizzaiola*, a pork sausage into which onion, tomato and other vegetables are mixed.

Beef

Grazing a steer takes a lot of pasture, and Sicilian beef production was never very impressive. It is interesting that in many countries, including the United States where beef production was always substantial, more pork than beef was consumed into the 1950s.

Several historical realities explain why there are more traditional beef recipes in Sicily than recipes for pork. The most obvious is the Muslim and Jewish presence in the Middle Ages.

Offal is popular in Sicily. *Pane con la milza* (a spleen sandwich) is a good example. Now there are also *spiedini* (shish kebabs) and *involtini* (stuffed beef rolls). The Sicilian variation of the *rollò,* a large cutlet rolled into a tube and stuffed with vegetables, is *falsomagro*. In Sicily it is stuffed with sausage, onions, cheese and eggs. Another Sicilian specialty is *bollito* (boiled beef). *Vitello al marsala* (veal marsala) is distinctly Sicilian, and meatballs, though less popular today than in the past, are part of the native cuisine.

Ovines

Until the mass industrialization of Italy's beef industry after 1950, sheep and goat were the mainstays of Sicilian meats. While these might be roasted in a kind of barbecue, they were often baked in an oven with potatoes, onions, tomatoes and other vegetables. Nowadays mutton (mostly lamb) and *capretto* (kid) are popular around Easter. Sheep brain is an esoteric delicacy. *Stigghiola* are the roasted intestines of sheep or goat, although beef calf intestines are sometimes used.

Rabbit

In Sicily, this creature is referred to as a *lepre,* or hare, when it's wild and hunted. The smaller, domesticated rabbit is simply a *coniglio.*

The term *al cacciatore* refers to rabbit roasted with vegetables. This recipe varies by region; in the southeast it is prepared with capers. "Chocolate rabbit" has unsweetened, grated Modican chocolate sprinkled over it, or blended into a sauce.

Poultry

Traditionally this was chicken. Partridge and grouse are sometimes hunted, and pigeon is occasionally, though rarely, consumed in Sicily. In the days of yore Sicilians feasted on all manner of birds, even starlings. Turkey has become popular and there are now farms that raise ostrich.

Pollo allo spiedo is chicken on a skewer. Our recipe chapter includes a traditional stuffing for baked chicken.

CHAPTER 10

Desserts and Pastries

"God gives biscuits to those without teeth."

— Sicilian Proverb

A meal should end at least as well as it begins, but Sicily's seemingly endless array of pastries, ice creams, coffees and other delights can be enjoyed any time. In a departure from tradition, we'll begin with the coffee.

Coffee

A number of Sicilian establishments roast and grind coffee beans into something suitable for brewing but coffee itself is not, strictly speaking, an Italian drink. Coffee, from the *coffea arabica* berry, first made its way into Europe commercially in the seventeenth century, and the Venetians were probably the first Italians to appreciate it. The coffee plant is native to Ethiopia, and late in the nineteenth century several Italian companies began to import it directly in large quantities. This profitable trade remained fairly steady even throughout some infamous Italian misadventures which briefly disturbed Italy's commerce in the region, most notably military debacles in Ethiopia in 1896 and again in 1941.

If you ask for a normal *caffé,* you'll get a strong, dense *espresso,* a term used rather rarely by Italians because that's the way coffee is normally served here. Incidentally, Italians usually serve coffee in what they call a *bar,* even if it resembles a French café. (The difference between the Italian pronunciation of *caffé* and *café* is too subtle to explain here.)

A *caffé* that is slightly diluted is *lungo,* and one that is denser than normal is *stretto.* If it has a few drops of steamed cream or milk in it, it's *macchiato.* An *espresso* with twice the strength and volume of an ordinary, small cup is a *doppio* (double). This may look like a *lungo* but it's not. Typically, Italians indulge in these *espresso* coffees on the run, standing at a crowded coffee bar. There's no dearth of these in Sicily. In the largest cities they seem to be everywhere, and in Palermo more so than in Catania.

Cappuccino is so-called because its light brown color is similar to that of the habits worn by Capuchin monks. This is similar to an *espresso lungo* topped off with hot, foamy milk and perhaps a sprinkling of chocolate. In Italy, this is a breakfast or mid-morning drink. Only foreigners ever drink it after noon, and some bars turn off the steam apparatus by lunchtime.

Caffé latte is an *espresso* with fresh milk that is poured on top but not steamed into a froth. It's a little heavier than a *cappuccino* but, like that coffee, usually a morning drink. Some purists consider *caffé latte* a children's drink. If you ask for a "latte" you are likely to get just that, plain milk.

An *americano,* as its name implies, is similar to the typical American cup of coffee. Even an American should never ask for this. Few Italian bartenders can or will make it.

A *caffè corretto* is an *espresso* served with a spoonful of amaretto, grappa or other dry spirit.

Caffè freddo (cold coffee) is more popular in Sicily than in other parts of Italy. This unique summer drink is coffee that is literally frozen into a granular substance which is almost — but not quite — liquid. Its consistency is a bit like that of granita.

Granita

The Italian word *granita* is often translated "frozen ice." That's a simplification, for granita is neither (as its name seems to imply) "granular" nor crushed ice. It consists of thin flakes of ice flavored with fresh fruit and sweetened with sugar.

Why the confusion? Outside Italy it used to be common to sell granular crushed ice — from cubes or even large blocks of solid ice — made with artificial flavors formulated with sweetened syrups as something akin to granita. The kinship was a distant one.

So how is real granita made?

Cold water, chopped fresh fruit (and its juice) and sugar are placed in a vat and the mixture is slowly churned at freezing temperatures until the flakes are formed. Then the granita must be churned continuously, and slowly so that it doesn't solidify into a block. As you can imagine, there are granita machines to do this work.

In the old days ice was scraped off of large blocks into flakes. It was never simply crushed.

The modern process offers the benefit of the fruit juice and pulp being infused into the ice flakes. Berries and citrus are the most common flavors. Lemon granita is literally bittersweet. Strawberry is popular, and mulberry, *gelsi* in Italian, is a rare delight.

Of course, hardly anybody chews granita. The ice flakes melt on your tongue. There's no need to suck on them.

Sicilian ice cream differs from granita in that it contains milk or cream, and perhaps some starch. In earlier times ice cream was made from snow. The origins of granita are closer to those of sorbet, which is icy but has a very fine consistency.

Gelato

Most agree that it's delicious, but the origins of Sicilian *gelato* (ice cream) have been debated for many years. Some theories support a Greek or Roman creation, others an Arab one. First, let's consider what separates *gelato* from other frozen desserts.

Ice creams are usually made from fruit, nuts, or even flowers (jasmine is a classic Sicilian flavor). Ice cream of the kind typically served in France, England and Russia is usually made with cow's milk or cream, and that's also true of most *gelati*. Sorbet is made without milk, and many fruit-based gelati (as opposed to those made from chocolate, coffee or nuts) fall into this category.

So why does Italian ice cream taste different from other ice creams? Even the creamiest *gelati* are rarely more than six or seven percent cream, while those of other countries may contain as much as twenty percent cream. In its most traditional recipe, the whipped American product known as "frozen custard" (ancestor of "soft" ice cream) may contain more than twenty percent heavy cream as well as eggs.

Gelato usually contains less emulsifier than other ice creams. Unlike other ice creams, *gelato* is not mixed at high speeds, and it is cooled differently. This creates a softer texture. Nowadays, the distinctions between one frozen dessert and another are often quite subtle. Certain English ice creams taste like Italian *gelato* and vice versa.

Where did gelato come from? Based on historical records, it is believed that in ancient Greek or Roman days foot runners brought snow from Mount Etna to Taormina or Catania to be flavored with nuts or berries and honey. It was a treat reserved for aristocrats. In the ninth century the Arabs introduced sugar cane, and this revolutionised Sicilian cooking. Before the ninth century local honey was used to sweeten Sicilian ices and sorbets.

Every part of Europe makes ice cream slightly differently. In Sicily carob flour is sometimes used to thicken ice cream. Indeed, in Sicily carob is raised almost exclusively for this purpose.

There are three ways to serve Sicilian ice cream. A large cup is a *spongato*. The cone is obvious. The *brioche,* or "ice cream sandwich," is *gelato* served in a sweet roll.

Modican Chocolate

Chocolate (possibly from *xocolatl* in the Aztec language), the product of cacao, the fruit of the cocoa tree, made its way into Europe — through Spain — during the sixteenth century. The granular chocolate made by the Aztecs bore little resemblance to the emulsified product developed in England by John Cadbury in the nineteenth century, but it was the Aztec chocolate that was introduced in Spanish Sicily.

The Spaniards ruled the Kingdom of Sicily from the War of the Vespers (in 1282) until the eighteenth century. The Spanish influence over the island led to the introduction of various fruits and vegetables discovered in the Americas, things like tomatoes, potatoes and tobacco.

Sicily's chocolate-making center was — and is — Modica, near Ragusa. It was probably introduced in connection with the influence of the Cabrera family, which held Modica as a fief into the early decades of the sixteenth century. The Cabrera were originally Catalonian. Though they had lived in Sicily for centuries, they maintained their close ties to Spain. It was unsurprising that Anna Cabrera, heir of John Cabrera, count of Modica, wed a Castilian admiral, Frederick Enriquez.

Little is known of Enriquez, but his exploits took him to the Americas, and he was probably the one who introduced chocolate production in Sicily.

This, of course, was a "cold" process very different from Cadbury's, which used heat. To this day, Modican chocolate adheres to the original Aztec recipe and has a very granular texture. Another Aztec characteristic is the addition of flavors such as vanilla and hot red pepper. Both of these crops were brought to Europe from the Aztec culture; Hernando Cortez introduced a drink made from cocoa and vanilla. Only later did vanilla become popular as a flavor unto itself.

Another "condiment" sometimes added to Modican chocolate is dried orange rind.

Today Sicily is one of the few places where Aztec-type chocolate is made (a firm in Spain has also preserved the tradition). Made from pure cocoa powder, it contains less of the natural fat (cocoa butter and chocolate liquor) and none of the additives of "modern" chocolate except sugar. It its purest form, it is invariably dark and contains no milk.

Modican chocolate, which has its own definition in European Union law, is readily ground or crushed for flavoring milk or pastries. It is also the flavoring for chocolate rabbit, a specialty in Malta and Ragusa. Yes, it is roasted rabbit covered in an unsweetened chocolate sauce. Grated Modican chocolate sprinkled over caponata makes that cold salad "Baroque." The point here is that chocolate wasn't always a sweet confection. In former times it was a versatile flavor.

Moderate servings of dark chocolate are healthy for your

heart, and the chocolate of Modica is dark chocolate in its purest form.

If you're a chocolate connoisseur you owe it to yourself to try it at least once.

Marzipan

The almond marzipan pastry known in Palermo as "Martorana Fruit" makes its annual debut late in the year when Autumn is upon us, usually in late October. This is traditional because of two annual occurrences, namely the harvesting of almonds (in early September) and the first "cool" days and nights (always a relative term in sunny Sicily) in October. The marzipan is usually on display in pastry shops by All Saints Day, celebrated on the first of November as an Italian national holiday. By tradition, it was a gift given to children on All Souls Day.

Martorana Fruit has a bit of an identity crisis. In Palermo it's named for the Martorana monastery, for reasons we'll explain, while elsewhere it's called *pasta reale* or even *frutta reale,* the Italian word *reale* meaning both real and royal.

Almond marzipan probably came to Sicily from Spain, where the Arabs may have introduced it during the Middle Ages. Whether they also brought it to Sicily, which was home to several emirates before 1071, is a matter of debate. The Arab almond marzipan is *lozina.* Similar pastries are known in Spain, Portugal, Greece and Cyprus. In antiquity, almond marzipan was probably first made in Persia or what is now Turkey.

The Martorana church began its life as a place of worship for Palermo's Greek Orthodox community during the twelfth century, but by the sixteenth century it was part of a monastic complex run by an order of nuns. Across southern Europe the nuns of the larger religious orders often made and sold various kinds of pastries. Marzipan, which also includes the sticky white "almond milk," should not be confused with the soft cookies made with almond paste. Marzipan is not a cookie.

Surprisingly little is known of marzipan's history in Sicily. The story about the Martorana's nuns shaping and decorating the marzipan to resemble fruit, then hanging it from dormant fruit trees to impress a bishop visiting one Easter, may well be an urban legend. Even so, it makes for an interesting one. Easter culminates the marzipan season. You won't find much Martorana Fruit in Sicily after April.

The pastry called *persipan,* which you won't find in Sicily, is made in cooler climates where almonds don't thrive, using peach or apricot kernels. In fact, these common fruits are closely related to the more aristocratic almond, and their edible if bitter kernels (the center of the pit) substitute for almonds in the manufacture of products such as "almond" soap.

There are two things to consider in the quality of Martorana Fruit. Firstly, it should not be too sweet. That may seem counterintuitive, but this is one show where sugar is not the star. Nowadays most Sicilian marzipan available commercially contains too much sugar. Worse yet, it is usually refined white sugar rather than the tastier, brownish, unrefined variety.

Next is the question of what might be called aesthetics or "design." In other words, the marzipan as a work of art. The best pasta reale is formed into shape using custom-made moulds which pastry-makers guard jealously and then "painted" to resemble actual fruit as realistically as possible. Yes, *pasta reale* may indeed mean "realistic paste." Even those who get the recipe and method right may fail when it comes to the decorating because, after all, not all pastry chefs are competent artists.

In the end, Martorana Fruit isn't just tasty pastry. It's art.

Cannoli

It is probably the best-known Sicilian pastry. The *cannolo,* a crust filled with cream, takes its name from its long tubular shape and has been prepared for centuries. The cheese cream used to fill cannoli is sweetened with sugar, and is based on a recipe very similar to that used to make the cream for *cassata.*

The term *cannolo* comes to us from a diminutive form of *canna* (a cane-like reed), such as a sugar cane stalk. In medieval times the tubular shell shape was formed by rolling the paste into a flat, circular shape, then wrapping it around a sugar cane stalk. A finger-size miniature version is now called the *sigaretta* (cigarette). Legends abound, but it appears that *cannoli* were invented in western Sicily, probably in Palermo or its vicinity. They became a springtime item, associated with Fat Tuesday (Carnevale) because the sheep produce more milk for ricotta in the spring when their grazing pastures are green. Spring is still the best time to buy "pecorino" (sheep) ricotta in Sicily.

In theory, the crust should be very thin, and the best pastry makers prepare it that way. Thicker tubes are easier to make and fry. Yes, the crusty shells are deep fried to achieve a crispy result, though nowadays some bakers prefer to bake them in an oven. Some commercial bakers coat the inside of the shells with chocolate. That's because they are filling them with cream hours or even days before serving. (Avoid this temptation; chocolate corrupts the flavor.) Ideally, the tubes should be filled immediately before serving, and the cream should be cold but not too close to freezing temperature.

Traditionally, cannoli are made with fresh ricotta cheese from sheep's milk. Ricotta from cow's milk has a different (milder) flavor. *Mascarpone,* a poor substitute which is less tasty but higher in fat, is not recommended.

Small pieces of candied fruits, particularly lemon, orange, citron and cherry, are sometimes mixed into the cream. Some chefs prefer pistachios or chocolate chips (too often a culinary crutch).

A new, slightly heretical, trend is the *cannolo scomposto,* the ricotta cream served separately from the shell, pieces of which the diner may dip into it. To us, this seems a bit like separating an Oreo cookie from its cream filling. Different strokes for different folks.

Cassata

The culinary dictum that "simpler is better" may reflect current realities, but some of life's tastiest treats are rather involved, and certainly time-consuming, from the standpoint of preparation. One of these delightfully tempting specialties is *cassata,* a Sicilian dessert which might be considered the king of Sicilian pastries.

Cassata is a tort of plain white cake filled with the same ricotta cream used in cannoli and sfinci, topped with frosting and sugared fruits. It is traditionally a Winter and Spring dessert served around Easter; in Sicily sheep produce little milk in summer, and frostings would melt under our island's torrid heat.

Its name is believed to derive from the medieval Arabic *kas'at* in reference either to its circular form (more precisely the pan used to mold it) or the word *cascio* for cheese.

One of the earliest "modern" references to *cassata* was a document issued at Mazara in 1575 mentioning its importance at religious feasts. *Cassata* probably originated at Palermo or another city of western Sicily.

There are two types of cassata. The most traditional form is a simple crust filled with cream, *cassata al forno.* The frosted form we have described is *barocca* or "baroque."

A local variation in the Madonie Mountains is *sfoglia madonita,* made with caciocavallo cheese instead of ricotta cream.

Cassata is the holiday dessert traditional to Sicily that panettone once was to northern Italy. It so happens that panettone is now made industrially and it has become popular throughout Italy.

Buccellato

December is *buccellato* time. In times past, dried fruits signalled the preparation of winter delights like fruit cake and plum pudding. Sicily's version is *buccellato,* a combination of figs, raisins, dates, nuts (usually almonds) and candied citrus like fruits like citron — all local Sicilian products — baked in a wreath-shaped cookie shell or as small pastries. But buccellato is much more than a simple fruit cake or fig pie.

Like many pastries, buccellato's origins are obscured by the mists of time. Nobody knows exactly when Sicilians began making it. In centuries past, honey was the sweetener. But every part of Europe has some kind of winter pastry made from dried fruits.

While it is associated with the harvest and cooler months, nowadays some pastry chefs make buccellato all year round. Well, if you can have strawberries in January, why not *buccellato* in June?

By tradition, *buccellato* was associated with family milestones. Godparents might give one to the parents of their godchild, or a marriage witness (best man or maid of honor) might give one to the parents of the bride. The point is that *buccellato* not only represented the good fortune and prosperity of the harvest, it was a very "rich" food in itself.

Today *buccellato* is most often associated with the Christmas holidays. The more common "national" Italian pastry of the Holiday season — which originated with Lombard and Piedmontese pastry makers "up north" — is *panettone,* a sweet but very plain, spongy bread cake made industrially and sold in cardboard cartons. There is no such thing as "assembly line" buccellato. It is still made by hand.

There is no single recipe for *buccellato*. Some versions call for jam, others for the addition of Marsala wine, itself a Winter favorite in Sicily. Almost any kind of nut can be used: almonds, hazelnuts, walnuts. The cake can be frosted or simply glazed and decorated with candied fruits.

Plum pudding by any other name.

Cuccìa

Particularly in Italy, certain foods are associated with certain feasts and occasions. Sicily is not unique in this regard — Americans' Thanksgiving turkey comes to mind — but it is certainly a good example.

Sicily's answer to rice pudding is something called *cuccìa,* based on a rather similar recipe but made with wheat grain — or "wheat berries" as they are commonly known. Only in early December, for the feast of Saint Lucy, are you likely to find *cuccìa* in Sicily. On her feast day (December 13th), few restaurants, pizzerias or pastry bars in Sicily serve baked wheat products, and some bakeries may be closed. Those eateries that are open serve cuccìa and rice balls (arancini).

Saint Lucy is the patroness of Siracusa. The *cuccìa* marks her saving the island from starvation in 1643, when a ship arriving in port loaded with grain was commandeered and its cargo seized to feed the people. They didn't bother grinding the wheat into flour, but simply boiled it. Historians debate whether that famine and others resulted more from a bad season or from poor administration of Sicily's agriculture and markets by greedy landlords, but that's another story.

Of course, wheat grains differ from rice grains, even in Italy. *Especially* in Italy, it may be said. The world's creamiest, most tender rice is something called *arborio* grown for centuries in Italy's Piedmont region and used in *risotto* and *arancini*. It is well-suited to rice pudding. Wheat berries, on the other hand, remain somewhat firm even after extensive boiling, never achieving the texture of rice or creating much of a cream. The point is that, unlike rice pudding, cuccìa owes most of its flavor and creaminess to the milk and cream used in its preparation, rather than the wheat grains. Incidentally, the fact that the durum ("hard") wheat cultivated in southern Italy is especially firm — better suited to farina for pasta than anything else — only adds to the strange texture of wheat pudding.

Cuccìa recipes include milk, cream, sugar, corn starch and vanilla. One might add a few small cubes of dried citron to the mixture just before chilling it. In recent years some "creative" pastry chefs have decided to add chocolate, or even take a shortcut and mix the boiled berries with the sweet ricotta cheese filling used in *cannoli*. That is a heresy of which Saint Lucy would never approve.

Sfinci

Sfinci (or *sfingi*, the singular is *sfincia*) are fried pastry puffs filled with ricotta-based cream similar to that used in making *cannoli* and *cassata*.

The Sicilian *sfincia* is similar to the Neapolitan *zeppola*, but the pastry is lighter and the cream filling typical of Sicily. It is important that the puffs be fried, not baked, because it is interaction with the boiling oil that makes them hollow. Unlike similar pastries in other parts of Europe, *sfinci* contain no butter or beef fat.

It is true that certain authors identify sfinci, *cassata* and *cannoli* with Arab cuisine as it existed in medieval Sicily. There is no absolute certainty here. That the *sfincia* may have existed in some form before the Arab period is implied by the former practice of serving it topped with honey instead of filling it with cream.

Sfinci are generally considered a Winter item, perhaps because in times past Winter and Spring were the best seasons for milk production by sheep. In principle, the cream is supposed to fill the pastry, but lazy chefs sometimes spoon it onto the surface of the *sfincia* instead.

In southern Italy and Malta, *sfinci* and *zeppoli* have come to be associated with Saint Joseph's Day, celebrated on March 19th. In Sicily several towns have Saint Joseph as their patron saint, notably San Giuseppe Jato. Traditionally, Piana degli Albanesi and Monreale were famous for their *sfinci* and *cannoli*. Saint Joseph is generally more widely venerated in southern Italy than in the north.

In the New Testament, Joseph, a carpenter by profession, is the husband of Mary and the foster father of Jesus. Some scholars believe that Joseph had other sons as well, and they generally agree that he died long before the crucifixion of Jesus. Joseph is the patron saint of manual workers and craftsmen.

So many "new" pastries have been introduced in Sicily in recent years that in the wake of this culinary invasion it isn't always easy to find *sfinci,* even in winter, except in small towns. The best solution is to be in Sicily on Saint Joseph's Day.

A local variation popular in Scicli is the *testa di Turco,* literally "Turk's head," a sfincia shaped into the form of a turban. This probably alludes to the Turkish pirates who raided the nearby coast during the sixteenth and seventeenth centuries, but the locals prefer to identify it with the Normans' conquest of Sicily from the medieval Arabs.

Torrone

An enduring legend, perhaps based on a grain of fact, says that *torrone* (literally "big tower") was invented for a medieval wedding in the Italian city of Cremona, the candy's name based on its having been shaped into a tower as an aristocratic "wedding cake." This story does not preclude the more probable history of the confection, which some historians believe originated in ancient Greece or Rome.

It has also been suggested that the very word *torrone* derives from the Arabic *turun,* denoting a similar confection. This theory suggests a Sicilian introduction of *torrone* into Europe, via the Arabs in the twelfth century or earlier, though the Greek-and-Roman theory seems the more probable explanation. It is entirely possible that similar confections were invented during the same early period in China, Persia and the Mediterranean. The simple fact is that the confection's precise origin has been lost to time.

Torrone is a very simple nougat candy made from egg whites, honey, nuts (usually almonds) and — in some recipes — cane sugar. The recipes of several popular commercial candy bars, like Toblerone and Mars, are based on that of traditional Italian *torrone.* That's why the flavor of *torrone* seems familiar to many who try it for the first time after having tasted these other candies. The more honey (and the less cane sugar) that is mixed into the torrone, the softer the final product. The softer, honey-based version is the more traditional.

Almonds are widely grown in Sicily, where pistachios are also used in torrone. Of all the confections made in Sicily, *torrone* may be one of the oldest if, indeed, it was made by the ancient Greeks. The method of heating and mixing the ingredients is very important if the *torrone* is to be made successfully. The proportion of egg white to honey is particularly important.

Sicilians sometimes, incorrectly, use the phrase *torrone di mandorla* when referring to *cubaita,* or almond brittle. *Cubaita* is also made with sesame seeds.

In Palermo a multicolored torrone served in the Summer for the feast of Saint Rosalie is called *gelato di campagna.*

Pignoccata

This sweet confection, typical of southeastern Sicily, is called *struffoli* and *mustazzoli* elsewhere. It is made of deep fried balls of dough mixed with honey.

Chiacchiere

Popular at Carnevale, this is a crisp pastry made of flattened dough, sweetened with sugar. Also called *angel wings* in English, it is similar to French *bugnes* and German *raderkuchen*.

Pignolata di Messina

Not to be confused with *pignoccata,* this is a small, soft pastry made in northeastern Sicily and served stacked on a plate, the term *pignolata* being "collective."

Stuffed Pastries

A number of popular tarts and pies are made year after year but don't fall into any clear category. One of the most traditional are *minni di virgini,* virgin's breasts. Said to resemble the breasts of Saint Agatha, these are hemispheric and sometimes frosted.

Biscotti

At the outset we should explain that the word *biscotto* is much abused outside Italy, where it is often used to refer to a specific type of crunchy cookie. A *biscotto* is *any* cookie.

Recipes abound. The most popular are *reginelle,* crumbly cookies coated with sesame seeds, and *biscotti all'anice,* anise cookies, which begin soft and harden. *Taralli,* which usually contain citron, resemble small, circular doughnuts formed into a ring shape. *Mostazzoli* are semi-soft almond cookies served in November, and recipes vary around Sicily. These are not to be confused with the *mustazzuola,* the *biscotto di San Martino* served on Saint Martin's Day, which is hard and virtually flavorless. *Quaresimali* are crunchy lenten cookies containing almonds. They are similar to Tuscan *cantuccini.*

Ricci are made with ground almonds, sugar, egg whites and lemon zest.

Sugared Fruits

Various desserts are made directly from fruit or fruit preserves. Candied citron and orange are obvious examples. There is also *cotognata,* quince preserves.

Custards and Cold Desserts

Several chilled or frozen desserts besides ice cream are traditionally popular in Sicily. The misnamed "parfait" is a confection similar to ice cream but formed at a warmer temperature. A similar dessert is *semifreddo.* The more seasonal *gelo di melone* is a sweet watermelon gelatin.

Biancomangiare (blancmange) is a cream made with milk (or cream), sugar, starch and almonds. This should not be confused with the less Sicilian *panna cotta,* which is a simpler custard.

CHAPTER 11

Cheeses and Ricotta

"We reached the cave of the Cyclops, but he was out tending sheep, so we went inside and took stock of all that we could see. His cheese racks were full of cheeses."

— Homer, *Odyssey*

Purists, as well as the Italian Ministry of Health and the food labelling bureaucrats of the European Commission, will tell you that cheeses, by definition, are aged milk products. That excludes most ricotta (cottage cheese) and mozzarella, and perhaps even Greek feta, from the list. In other words, there's a difference between curd and cheese. With exceptions like soy cheese (which rather resembles tofu), all traditional cheeses are made from some form of milk, whether it's from a cow, a sheep or a goat.

Like wine and olive oil, traditional cheese is protected based on variety and region. In the European Union this standard is the *protected designation of origin* (PDO), which is applied in tandem with *protected geographical indication* (PGI). Gorgonzola, for example, is not merely any "blue" Italian cheese but that produced using a certain method in the eponymous town near Milan.

Cheese

What makes cheese different, apart from the source of the milk (and even the variety of cow, sheep or goat), is the culture and ageing process used in its manufacture. That's why ricotta differs from feta, though both are made from the milk of sheep or goats, and it's why English cheddar differs from Sicilian provola, both made from cow's milk. Even if the same method, culture and bovine species were used, Sicilian provola would still taste different from a hypothetical English variety because the livestock of both regions graze in different pastures, producing milk that tastes differently. This all seems slightly arcane, but it's good to know something about cheese making when comparing different varieties of cheese.

More Sicilian cheese is produced from cow's milk than from sheep's milk, but there are more sheep than cows in Sicily. Virgil and other classical writers mention the flourishing export market for Sicilian cheeses in Greece. Certain Sicilian cheeses made in ancient times are still made today, though others were introduced by the Arabs, Normans and Longobards during the Middle Ages.

The Italian government long ago established rigid standards defining particular varieties of cheese, and these norms are supported by the European PDO already mentioned. Prominent traditional successes are northern Italy's Parmesan and Gorgonzola, easily identified and protected. Here are some of the better known Sicilian cheeses.

Pecorino, as its name implies, is made from sheep's milk, *pecora* meaning sheep. It is true that Sicily's sheep population is diminishing, but in Italian regions, only Sardinia presently raises more sheep than Sicily. Like Tuma, Pecorino is sometimes flavored with peppercorns or other spices. Made throughout Sicily, where it may be considered the most widely produced aged cheese product, it is a favourite for grating over pasta. Its taste, though sharp, is often less pungent and dry than that of Caciocavallo, despite a distinctive flavor and texture (it crumbles and flakes easily).

Caciocavallo is made from cow's milk, though its cryptic name literally means "horse cheese," the Sicilian word *cacio* sharing the same root as *casein* while *cavallo* means horse. Nobody in Sicily has milked a mare lately, as far as we know. The cheese owes its name to the manner in which two pear-shaped bulbs of it were attached by a string, much like the balls of a bola, and suspended from a wooden beam "a cavallo" as though astride a horse; think of saddle bags. It takes at least eight months to age Caciocavallo properly, achieving a sharper flavor in about two years. Caciocavallo is a good complement to stronger wines, and widely used for grating over pasta. Indeed, it is a favourite of Sicilian chefs. Despite its interesting name, nowadays it is usually rectangular, purchased in thick slices. Caciovacchino was a similar product made in times past.

Canestrato is made from whole cow's milk, sometimes diluted with that of goats or sheep. Its name derives from its ageing in baskets (canestri). It is quite similar to Pecorino, made with the same process, and there is a theory that Canestrato was developed to obtain a similar product while using cow's milk. Its form is usually cylindrical, weighing as much as thirty pounds (about fifteen kilograms). It is usually somewhat sweet until aged more than fourteen months. Sicilians prefer to consume Canestrato as a table cheese with wine, fruit or both.

Piacentinu, famous in the province of Enna in central Sicily, is made from sheep's milk and flavored with saffron, which gives it a golden hue. The name comes from the Sicilian cognate of *piacere* (to like).

Provola, which comes in regional Sicilian varieties (Nebrodi, Ragusa, Madonie), is made from whole cow's milk. There's also a tasty smoked form, and it's the classical complement to hams. It assumes a sharp flavor when aged. Made using a very old method, Provola is usually formed into a bulb, then suspended from a ribbon or string for ageing. This gives it a pear shape, with each bulb weighing a kilogram or less. In general, the more mature the Provola, the deeper yellow its rind.

Tuma and its kindred Primo Sale are known, in some forms, as *Vastedda* in some parts of Sicily, such as the Belice Valley. Made from sheep's milk, it is usually called Tuma when served right out of the mould, Primo Sale when salted lightly, and Vastedda when aged slightly longer. Like Pecorino, Tuma is sometimes flavored with peppercorns or other spices. Unlike Pecorino, it does not age well and is best served with ham, wines and fruits as a table cheese. It has a sweet taste not unlike that of Provola, with an equally rubbery texture.

Maiorchino, its name drawn from a term in a local dialect of northeastern Sicily, is made in the Peloritan and Nebrodi regions. It contains roughly equal amounts of whole milk from native breeds of cow, sheep and goat.

Ragusano, made from cow's milk, has a mild flavor. It is made in the province of Ragusa in southeastern Sicily.

Niche Cheeses: A number of other regional Sicilian cheeses are made from goat's or sheep's milk. Several that should be mentioned are *Capra* (Messina), *Fiore Sicano* (Palermo), *Cofanetto, Ericino* and *Caciotta degli Elimi* (Trapani), *Tumazzo Modicano* (Modica), and *Caciocavallo Ibleo* (Noto and Ragusa). In the Sicanian Mountains one finds *Tuma Persa.*

Ricotta

By definition, *ricotta* is an Italian type of cottage cheese, or "basket cheese." But it isn't really cheese. Like various "milk products" — feta, yogurt, mozzarella, sour cream, buttermilk and mascarpone come to mind — it fits into a specific category other than that of cheese. This is a question of ingredients but also of method, as most true cheeses (even creamy ones like brie and camembert) are at least slightly aged.

Then there is the matter of the source of the milk. Feta is made from goat's milk, mozzarella from the milk of cows or buffalo. Sicilian ricotta is made from sheep's milk, though it is possible to use cow's milk too. Because it is so simple to make, cottage cheese is made in certain parts of Asia and Africa where true cheese recipes are unknown in the local cuisine.

So while there are numerous Sicilian cheeses, ricotta isn't one of them. Most cheeses are made from "whole" milk and varying quantities of cream. When boiled, milk, consisting mostly of proteins such as casein, separates into solids and liquids. The liquid is mostly whey, or milk plasma. After straining, the solids, or curds, that remain are primarily casein. Several procedures exist to curdle milk or cream, and it's possible to use rennet or lemon juice, but ricotta is made by simple heating. The word *ricotta* itself literally means "re-cooked."

Ricotta actually contains more curds than whey, and its culinary category is "whey cheese" or "curd cheese." Some milk protein solids (casein) remain after straining, and a bit of salt is added to most ricotta. Sheep ricotta, called *ricotta di pecora,* is typically around fifteen percent fat.

A slightly aged version of ricotta is *ricotta salata* or *ricotta al forno,* which is a brick of dense, solidified (pressed) ricotta coated with salt. This effect is achieved by slowly baking and even smoking the pressed ricotta.

It is *ricotta di pecora* that gives the cream filling of cannoli, cassata and sfinci its very distinctive taste. Ricotta made from cow's milk just doesn't have the same flavor.

European standards dictate that ricotta must be made in stainless steel vats under specific conditions, but for traditional rustic atmosphere there's nothing like seeing it made outdoors, on a sheep farm.

Ricotta is "seasonal," with the best product made during the months that Sicily's pastures are greenest, from November through May, when the grazing sheep produce the most milk. As demand has increased, so has the price of "genuine" ricotta, and much of what is sold in Sicily today, especially during the warmer months, is made from a mixture of sheep's milk and cow's milk.

CHAPTER 12

Olives and Olive Oil

"This island that Zeus, the lord of Olympus, conceded to give Persephone, the pride of the blossoming earth."

— Pindar, *The Odes*

Carolea, Nocellara, Biancolilla. Their names roll off your tongue. It's difficult, indeed inconceivable, to consider Sicilian cuisine without thinking about Sicily's olive oil.

In the Beginning

Sicily's olive varieties trace their origins on our island from time immemorial, with the first wild oleasters and (much later) varieties like the Greek *kalamata,* probably the first domesticated cultivar brought to Sicily – preserved today as a single ancient tree in the southeastern part of our island. Sicilian olive oil is among the world's most fragrant and appetizing. To categorize it generically among "Italian olive oils," as though you were filling out a customs declaration, is to overlook its unique qualities.

It is believed that Sicily's particularly fertile soil, which in eastern regions is volcanic, produces some of the world's best olives.

The ancient Athenians preferred Sicilian olive oil to their own, though some of the varieties grown in Sicily and Greece were actually the same. Over the last two decades, olive oils made in the Hyblaean Mountains of southeastern Sicily have been served at Buckingham Palace and the White House, but every region of the island produces delicious oil.

A Question of Color

The question of color should be put to rest. A persistent perception holds that the greener its color, the purer the olive oil. This is generally true for most varieties of olive oil, but it must be said that certain varieties of olive yield a slightly more golden oil.

Like grapes, olives come in different colors. Olives may be green, gray or black when ripe, depending on the variety. Curing does not alter the basic color of the olives, but only deepens it. Certain types of olive tree grown in Calabria's Aspromonte region are tall and thin, producing a small dark fruit from sparse branches. The Sicilian trees are usually shorter with somewhat dense foliage. This makes it easier to pick the olives by hand, which causes less damage to the trees than mechanical harvesting.

Pressing Method

There are several ways of pressing olives to draw the oil out of them, and in the public mind there's a lot of confusion about categories. Here are the European Union's grading standards.

Extra Virgin Olive Oil: Cold pressing uses a natural process, with little or no heat (under 27 degrees Celsius, or 80 F), to extract the first oil from the freshly harvested olives. This product is extra virgin olive oil. Pure olive oil from freshly-harvested olives. No other grade of oil is added. When it is unfiltered, it has a cloudy consistency and a grayish sediment. To purists, this is the best grade of olive oil, and it is ideal for salads. However, the extra virgin olive oil sold in stores is usually filtered, and beware of "extra virgin" oils produced outside the European Union, where the term may be defined less rigorously. Italian extra virgin olive oil must have an acidity level no greater than one percent. It is most fragrant right after pressing.

Virgin Olive Oil: Unless labelled "cold pressed," this olive oil may be slightly "refined," meaning that it is extracted with a heat process. Though derived principally from whole olives, it may also contain some oil extracted from the husks (pomace) that remain following the initial "cold" pressing employed in producing *extra* virgin oil. And chemical agents may be used. But despite the process used to obtain it, this is pure olive oil, even if its acidity level is relatively high and its taste unexceptional.

Olive Oil: Oil sold under this generic designation need only derive the greater part of its volume from olives and olive pomace. It is not necessarily pure. Other vegetable oils may be added! And what olive oil is present is extracted using chemical agents and heat. This mediocre category also includes *lampante* oils (see *Caveat Emptor* below).

Organic Oils: In theory, these may be virgin or extra virgin, but we recommend the latter. To be designated *organic,* an Italian olive oil must be made from olives grown on trees which have been free from chemical agents for at least three years. This conforms to European and Italian national directives.

Commercial Classifications: Here an example is the vaguely defined product called "light" olive oil, a marketing gimmick that permits firms to sell low grade, less flavorful olive oil as though it were better for your health or tastier in recipes. These are misleading claims because research has shown that pure extra virgin olive oil (whatever its geographic source) is one of the best oils you can consume. Why would any chef prepare a salad using a bland product that doesn't taste like traditional cold-pressed, extra virgin olive oil?

Quality

Apart from its purity and the extraction process used to produce it, olive oil is distinguished by its acidity. In general, the lower the acidity, the better the oil.

Olive oil is also graded by its density, or viscosity, though this does not imply a judgement of its culinary quality. Unfiltered oil is naturally denser, and more opaque, than filtered oil. The first seasonal pressing, available by early December, is sold in much the same way as Novello wine. When olives are pressed, the pits (stones) are crushed as well, and this yields a better oil.

By Any Other Name

Italy is one of the world's largest producers of olive oil, but olive varieties are not identical. Several traditional olive varieties have been grown in Sicily for a very long time, and are preferred to hybrids, of which there are many.

Verdello is a large green olive. Biancolilla is favored in southwestern Sicily, Nocellara Messinese and Ogliarola Messinese in the northeast. Crasto is grown in the lowlands of the Madonie Mountains of northern Sicily. Cerasuola (Ogliara) is raised in the vast area between Sciacca and Paceco. La Minuta is grown in the area of Patti and Capo d'Orlando in the province of Messina. La Cavaleri is raised in the Caltagirone area, Biancolilla around Agrigento. The Tonda Iblea variety is raised around Ragusa, while Moresca is grown in the triangular zone formed by Catania, Siracusa and Ragusa. Castiglione is native to the volcanic Alcantara Valley near Taormina. Nocellara del Belice is raised in the Trapani area, Carolea in the Enna region. Some varieties are better for salads, others for pressing. Castiglione, Biancolilla, and the various Nocellara varieties, for example, are better for pressing.

Appellation

In theory, like Sicilian wines, olive oils should carry an appellation indicating where the olives pressed to make it were grown, but very few actually do. Most Sicilian chefs select oils by variety rather than appellation. While the law favors appellations by region over the varieties of olives used to make the oil, there are guidelines for these, so a Valle del Belice oil should be made primarily from olives traditionally typical of that area. European norms such as *protected designation of origin* (PDO) seek to prevent usurpation of names identified with specific regional products. Appellations follow (the map indicates these).

Colline Ennesi. Hilly region around Enna in east-central Sicily, generally contiguous to that province. Carolea is the principal variety.

Colli Nisseni. Mountainous region around Caltanissetta in eastern Sicanian Mountains. Carolea and Biancolilla are the chief varieties.

Monte Etna. As the name implies, the areas on the slopes of Mount Etna, fruits of its rich volcanic soil. The range of varieties includes Nocellara Etnea, Moresca, Tonda Iblea, Ogliara Messinese, Biancolilla, Brandofino and Castiglione.

Monte Iblei. Region of the Hyblaean Mountains of southeastern Sicily. Preferred varieties are Tonda Iblea, Moresca and Nocellara Etnea.

Valdemone. Generally contiguous to the province of Messina, including much of the Nebrodi region. Various varieties including Ogliarola Messinese, Verdello, La Minuta, Nocellara Messinese, Ottobratica, Brandofino and Verdello.

Valle del Belice. The Belice Valley south of Trapani, principally Nocellara olives but also Biancolilla, Cerasuola (Ogliara), Buscionetto (Biancolilla), Santagatese.

Val di Mazara. Southwestern area. Preferred varieties are Biancolilla, Cerasuola, Nocellara del Belice.

Valle dei Templi. The area in the immediate vicinity of Agrigento. Principal varieties are Biancolilla and Cerasuola (Ogliara).

Valli Trapanesi. Large region around Trapani in western Sicily's wine country. Principal varieties are Cerasuola and Nocellara del Belice.

Caveat Emptor

A few years ago, we received an email from an American importer of olive oil asking why we never mentioned his favorite brand as one of Sicily's best. Here our candor gave way to diplomacy. We didn't have the heart to inform him that — apart from considerations of flavor — the olive oil he imported from Sicily was not made from Sicilian olives.

Yes, some Sicilian firms use olives from Calabria, Apulia or other parts of Italy to make the oil they press in Sicily. Indeed, many of the best known "Italian" olive oils, even those classified "virgin," are actually produced from olives imported from Spain, the Balkans, Turkey and Tunisia. None of this is illegal, just slightly misleading.

While much of the "Sicilian" olive oil sold in the export market is, in fact, made from locally-grown olives, under European Union law there's little accountability for the precise origin of the product. In some cases the olives are pressed abroad (outside Italy) and the oil is imported into Italy for bottling as "Mediterranean" oil with little regard for precise extraction standards or quality.

Much is *lampante,* an oil pressed from dried, dirty olives found on the ground rather than harvested from the trees. Most *lampante* is also "rectified" with chemical agents in order to control its acidity; sometimes such oil is extracted using talc. There are virtually no import controls for oil which arrives in Italy from other EU countries. A highly controversial 1995 law permits much *lampante* oil to be sold as "virgin." The result of this deceptive labeling is that, incredibly, much of the olive oil sold in Italy is not Italian, and it may not even be pure olive oil.

Olive Products

The oil is only one of the products of the olive. There is also green, grey or black olive paté, a delightful spread for sandwiches or appetizers. And, of course, there are both cured and dried olives. Some firms market their own oils, pressed from olives grown on their own farms. More often, the company that bottles and sells the oil has purchased the harvests of numerous growers.

CHAPTER 13

Wines of Sicily

"The wine of Taormina enjoys a high repute, and flagons of it are sometimes passed off for Mammertine wine. Messina nowadays exports wines of good quality which age well."

— Pliny the Elder, *Natural History*

When it comes to wine, *Sicilia* is no dilettante. Sicilians have been making wine for around three thousand years.

The wine country of western Sicily is one of Italy's largest contiguous viticultural regions. It saw its greatest growth with the popularity of Marsala wine during the early decades of the nineteenth century, when viticulture replaced the cultivation of wheat in these areas. (We'll meet Marsala in our next chapter.)

Then and Now

Vines, of course, have been cultivated in Sicily since antiquity. Until the twentieth century, however, most of the wine consumed in Sicily was home made and not of a very high quality compared to today's estate-bottled vintages. Much of it was rather high in alcohol content and neither red or white but a light amber color.

In Sicily red wines were historically more popular than whites. The quintessentially Sicilian Nero d'Avola is the most robust of these. Sicily, where there is rarely a cloudy day from June through August, hardly ever produces a mediocre harvest, and as early as the nineteenth century some of its growers were selling Nero d'Avola in bulk as a blending grape to wineries in France to add color and body to wines deemed lacking in those qualities — this is one of those wine industry secrets that are so incredible as to leave aficionados agape, not knowing whether it should be believed. (This trade in "cutting wine" began when the phylloxera epidemic decimated France's vineyards in the 1860s.)

The island has several regional wine appellations but thus far only those of the dessert wines have achieved international prestige among oenophiles, and the Sicilians themselves purchase their wines according to variety rather than geography. Most of the appellations, in Italian officialese *denominazioni di origine controllata,* do not correspond to grape varieties, so one sees *Bianco d'Alcamo* promoted as if it were a varietal (rather than a white from western Sicily), and in practice the *denominazioni* are generally ignored. Nevertheless, European legislation reinforces Italian standards with *protected designation of origin* (PDO) and *protected geographical indication* (PGI).

Italians consume a fair amount of wine *per capita.* Socially, alcohol consumption is moderate. Anybody who spends much time in Sicily will probably notice how rare alcoholism is among the Sicilians. Public insobriety is all but unknown, and very few automobile accidents result from drunk driving. Social culture is often cited in explanation of this, but genetic factors may be at work too.

Syrah and Chardonnay seem to have conquered a good part of the world, but Sicily's robust reds and distinctive whites make for a fine complement to any meal.

Wild grapes thrived on our island long before the arrival of the Mycenaeans and others. However, it was only with the great influx of Greek colonists around 700 BC (BCE) that higher quality vines and better methods of cultivation were widely introduced.

The most famous ancient wines were Mamertino (probably introduced by a group of mercenaries at Milazzo around 270 BC), Tauromenio (of Taormina), and Pollio (in the area of Syracuse). Sicilian wines were also greatly appreciated by the ancient Romans, and this fact is mentioned by Pliny the Elder. Julius Caesar loved Mamertino wine, which is still produced in the area of Milazzo.

Pollio wine was named after a Greek tyrant of Syracuse, Pollis of Argos, who introduced this variety to Sicily, and today it is known as *Moscato Siracusano*.

During the centuries following the fall of the Roman Empire, Sicilian viticulture underwent a crisis period. That began to change with the arrival of the Arabs, who increased grape cultivation. This they did to produce raisins, which made their way into the local cuisine, but medieval chroniclers mention that by the eleventh century the island's Muslims were known to consume wine on occasion.

However, it was not until the fifteenth century that Sicilian wines started to be exported to northern Italy, and this reached its climax thanks to the immense success of Marsala around 1800.

Wine Country

Grapes are raised in every part of Sicily, but the heart of the island's principal viticultural region will be found between Salemi and Marsala. More broadly, it extends from the suburbs of Marsala south-eastward toward Menfi, framed by the ancient Greek sites of Segesta and Selinunte, embracing localities such as Alcamo, Trapani and Castelvetrano. The larger cities are not without their charm, but it's the smaller towns and hamlets, with the occasional castle, *baglio* or farmhouse, that capture the imagination. And, of course, vineyards as far as the eye can see. The rolling hills planted with vines are themselves the main attraction; the mountains are merely a backdrop. Its a good place to breathe the tranquility of the real, rural Sicily of centuries past.

The most suggestive viticultural landscapes are elusive. Here's one of our favorite drives. From Salemi, take the SS 188 to Marsala. Along this route one encounters little traffic but an endless array of gently rolling hills carpeted with vineyards as far as the eye can see. It's a magical place that rivals any viticultural region in the world in its serene dignity. It also boasts a more distinguished history than most. Domesticated grapes were cultivated here long before they were introduced into France or northern Italy. Coming from Palermo, Segesta is a convenient stop near Salemi.

Survival

Unfortunately, like many other regions, beginning around 1880, Sicily was attacked by the phylloxera louse and most of the vines were destroyed. Only the ones on Mount Etna were spared due to the presence of sulfur in the local volcanic soil. Consequently, today the grapevines of Mount Etna are the oldest on the island.

In any case, before the phylloxera epidemic, there were numerous grape varieties in Sicily. Yet only a few families, such as the Alliatas (with their Corvo brand), were producing what we might call "estate-bottled" wine.

This fact is mentioned by Baron Antonio Mendola, a great Sicilian ampelographer and agronomist who lived into the early years of the twentieth century.

Nowadays in Sicily research is being conducted on ancient, forgotten grapevines.

A recent discovery was made regarding renowned Grillo grapes. It has been determined, in fact, that the Grillo variety was actually invented thanks to research developed by Mendola in 1874. He grafted Catarratto stock to either Zibibbo or Moscato in order to obtain a more fragrant Marsala wine.

Research in this field is still being conducted. The goal is to create new grape varieties through more grafting. This procedure renders grapevines more resistant to parasites and disease. Sicily has enormous potential for the production of excellent wines that is truly worth developing thanks to its exceptional climate and topographical diversity.

Here, in scrupulously fair, alphabetical order, is a list of some of the more important "native" Sicilian grape varieties.

Carricante (Catanese Bianco). A white from the Etna area.

Cataratto Bianco. A white traditional in the Trapani area and used in Marsala wine, characterised by a delicate flavor and medium alcohol level.

Corinto. A red grape used to make Passolina raisins; blended (five percent) to make Malvasia wine.

Frappato. Strong red of uncertain origin grown in southeastern Sicily. It is genetically very similar to Gaglioppo (see below).

Gaglioppo. A red of Calabrian origin frequently grown in Sicily. Similar to Frappato.

Grecanico (Greco). A white so-called for its Greek origins. Genetically very similar to the Garganega cultivated in Veneto.

Grillo. A distinctive white.

Insolia (Inzolia) or **Anzolia.** Used to create dry white table wines, either as a varietal or blended with varieties such as Chardonnay.

Malvasia. A muscatel sub-variety used to make the wine of this name.

Moscato. Muscat, a traditional variety widely used in Italy, in Sicily associated with the dessert wine of this name, similar to Malvasia. The muscatels are one of European winemaking's most widespread grape types.

Nerello. Strong red grown in two varieties, Mascalese and Cappuccio.

Nero D'Avola. Sometimes called "Calabrese," this is Sicily's most popular red grape, used in the region's bestselling varietal wine. In the past Nero d'Avola, like other Sicilian reds, was often syrupy, with an alcohol content reaching eighteen percent, rather high for a table wine. New viticulture techniques and night harvesting (placing the grapes in cooled vats to prevent premature fermentation) have been used by a few vintners to retain flavor without producing an overpowering wine. It takes a certain finesse to "harness" a grape with this much body; the Milazzo and Planeta wineries have achieved this.

Perricone (Pignatello). Esoteric, robust red which in the past was used to make Ruby Marsala.

Primitivo. This red grape of Balkan origin is called *Zinfandel* in America, rarely cultivated in Sicily today.

Zibibbo (Moscatellone). Sicily's muscatel mainstay is a sub-variety of Muscat of Alexandria. Owing its name to the Arabic *zabìb* (literally *raisin*), Zibibbo was much favored by the Fatimids, but the grape was probably introduced in Sicily — first on Pantelleria — by the Phoenicians, who brought cultivars from Egypt.

Novello

This is a category rather than a variety. The Italian "nouveau" reds of Autumn have become a surprisingly successful fixture in the wine industry. Here in Sicily, autumn means Saint Martin's Day, 11 November, with its traditional hard biscuits and fortified wines, as well as its association with what Italians call "Saint Martin's Summer." It's a little like the "Indian Summer" of North America, swept by the last warm breezes before the winter chill sets in — though in most parts of Sicily that chilly season is rather ephemeral, with wild artichokes harvested almost until Christmas and the almond trees already blossoming by mid-February. It is usually during the week before Saint Martin's Day that the first Novello (nouveau) wines make their appearance in Italy. With the minimal necessary fermentation time and little or no traditional ageing, they retain a robust yet fruity flavor, even when the heartiest grapes are used.

Novello refers to any "new" red of the current vintage, with a current bottling date. This is during early November, two weeks before the French government permits the sale of

Beaujolais Nouveau (the best known wine of this kind). In Italy, this implies harvesting a few weeks before the French grapes are ripe, and the earlier sale date is a potential marketing advantage for Sicilian vintners. Sicily's harvest is one of Europe's earliest. Under Italian law, Novello can be placed on sale as early as 6 November.

Like its French counterparts, Sicily's Novello is a low-tannin wine made using the process of carbonic maceration or "whole-berry fermentation." Essentially, this is a modern process that uses carbon dioxide (depriving the grapes of oxygen) to increase rapid alcohol production by the sugars present in the grapes, and then adding yeast to the must (pulp, juice and skin), bringing about fast fermentation. The result is a lighter red wine which lacks the tannins necessary for long storage in the bottle but tastes great. The Italian term *novello* has come into widespread international use to describe the wines made with this process, even for non-Italian products.

CHAPTER 14

Liqueurs, Spirits, Dessert Wines

"Surely the earth, giver of grain, provides the Cyclops with fine wine, and rain from Zeus does swell our clustered vines. But this is better, a wine as fragrant as ambrosia and nectar."

— Polyphemus, in Homer's *Odyssey*

A number of fortified and dessert wines, and various spirits, have been made in Sicily for centuries. Here we'll describe those that are most popular.

Marsala

Sicily's most famous wine was first made in the city that shares its name on the western coast by the Woodhouse firm, which also sold Port.

It is usually made from local grapes such as Grillo, Cataratto and Insolia — whites that can stand on their own as table wines. This wine, which travels well, was developed around 1800 for the British market, as the supply of Port, Sherry and Madeira was no longer sufficient to meet consumer demand. Much used in cooking, Marsala figures in some traditional Sicilian recipes, for example veal (and chicken) *al Marsala* and *zabaglione* (eggnog), both included in our recipe chapter.

Like its Spanish and Portuguese sisters, Marsala is a fortified wine with an alcohol content of around twenty percent by volume

For more than a century, Marsala was the equal of Sherry and Madeira, if not Port. By the 1950s, however, it found itself relegated to the kitchen as cooking wine, and by 1970 commercial competition had arrived from unexpected quarters, with the introduction of a "California Marsala" and even a "Marsala" made in the Finger Lakes region of New York state. The matter of European appellations lacking protection outside Europe is a complex one; our point is that there is really no adequate substitute for genuine Italian Marsala.

Wars have always sealed Marsala's fate. In the eighteenth century, as we mentioned in Chapter 2, it was the wars between Britain and Spain that motivated an Englishman to produce fortified wine in Sicily as an alternative to Spanish counterparts. Until the Second World War, Marsala was used more for drinking than cooking. The war interrupted export to Britain and the United States. In its aftermath, there was a glut of Marsala. In an effort to sell this supply, producers promoted it as a cooking wine.

In 1986, Italy's D.O. (denomination of origin or appellation) laws for Marsala were revised to incorporate stricter regulations similar to those which the Portuguese government instituted for Port (a somewhat heavier wine), and Marsala is now resuming its place as a dessert and aperitif wine.

Today's Marsala is often divided into three different standards, namely *oro* (golden), *ambra* (amber), and *rubino* (ruby). Some marsala makers prefer to categorize it according to terms used for Port wine, such as *tawny*.

There are both sweet and dry types, and various categories (of which we'll mention just a few). *Fine* is aged for a minimum of one year, while *Superiore* is aged for a minimum of two years (some vintners age it for three years). *Superiore Riserva* (often simply "Riserva") is a vintage wine aged in wood for four years, and sometimes as long as six. *Vergine* is aged in wood for a minimum of five years (some firms age it in small oak casks for as long as seven years).

For cooking, there's even a Marsala made with the addition of egg white (though you probably won't notice this ingredient). Truth be told, there are dozens of kinds of Marsala wine, some unique to certain houses, each meeting particular standards. Some estates age it in oak casks from the 1860s, making your Marsala experience a piece of Sicilian history. Marsala shouldn't be confused with other sweet Sicilian dessert wines of amber color, which we'll describe.

Some pleasant Marsala liqueurs have also been introduced, though they're difficult to find on the market. Almond-flavored Marsala, best described as Sweet Marsala with a touch of Amaretto, is a commercial attempt to exploit the market.

Zibibbo

The Zibibbo grape, which we met in the last chapter, is a Muscat variety historically used in the making of Moscato wine, which can also be made from the sub-variety known locally as Moscatello, sometimes with the addition of Corinto.

Purists will tell you that Zibibbo is a grape variety that can be used to make anything from table wine to grappa. That's true. However, the "Zibibbo" made commercially by several houses is a strong wine similar to Marsala but fermented and then partially distilled naturally, without the addition of spirits. The process differs also in that Zibibbo is actually made from grapes partially fermented in the sun. It is a very old process, and Zibibbo, though not the precursor of Marsala, derives from a formula known in the Middle Ages. It is typically slightly lower in alcohol than Marsala (about fifteen percent compared to eighteen or twenty percent) and sometimes more robust. The wine known as Moscato di Pantelleria Naturale is made mostly from Zibibbo grapes.

Moscato

The high-alcohol wine known as *Moscato* exists in its own little niche. It comes from the Muscat grape, of course, or from the sub-variety known locally as Moscatello, sometimes with the addition of Corinto or Zibibbo. Some fine whites can be made from Muscat, but in Sicily and the nearby islands Moscato is usually rendered as a golden or light amber dessert wine (popular with hard cookies on St Martin's Day), sometimes fortified or even sparkling (spumante). A few localities are famous for Moscato. Like Passito, it is made by some distinguished wineries on the islands of Pantelleria and Lipari.

Passito

As its name implies, Passito contains *Appassito* grapes. By tradition, vintners use a special "dry" process in production of Passito, so semi-dry grapes and even raisins find their way into the must. Unlike Marsala and Port, to which alcohol may be added, sweet Passito is not a "fortified" wine. This brings us to the point that *Passito* refers as much to a winemaking *process* as to a specific grape variety.

Malvasia

Malvasia is another white grape used to make a strong varietal that is golden to amber in color and slightly fortified. Bred from an older grape variety, Malvasia is grown in northeastern Sicily (near Messina) and on the island of Lipari, where it is used in the making of a wine somewhat similar to Moscato. Most Malvasia wines contain five percent Corinto, a local red.

Flavored Wines

There are several mildly fortified, flavored white wines which, though not suitable for every occasion, go well with some desserts. Those flavored with almonds are the most popular.

Liqueurs and Spirits

Grappa is a brandy distilled from grape seeds and pomace. Dry and high in alcohol, it is usually white (clear) and served as an after-dinner drink. In Italy, grappa is often sold in artistically original clear glass bottles which the distillers commission specially for this liquor. Like grappa, various liqueurs, were home made in the past.

Some are sweet, while others fall into the esoteric category of "bitters." Several that are unique to Sicily are worthy of mention. Ala, made by Florio, has a distinct flavor, as does Averna, which is made in Caltanissetta. Fichera, a newcomer, is made near Mount Etna.

Several Sicilian liqueurs are similar to those produced on the mainland, namely limoncello, from lemons, anisette (sambuca) and amaretto, from almonds. There are others, such as the interesting liqueur made from prickly pears, and Cynar, from artichokes.

Rosolio was traditionally made from rose petals. It is now an entire category of sweet liqueurs. That made from strawberries, for example, is sometimes called *rosolio di fragala*.

Liqueurs made from almonds, hazelnuts or walnuts add a nice touch when poured over a cup of vanilla ice cream.

CHAPTER 15

Culinary Festivals

"Zeus divided the year into halves, and now the goddess Persephone, a deity belonging to two worlds, spends the same amount of time each year with her mother and with her husband."

— Ovid, *Metamorphoses*

What, exactly, are we talking about? Certainly, Sicilians don't need a folk festival to enjoy good food. But in the course of a year it is the festivals that signal the changes in the seasons.

By tradition, a *festa* was a religious observance. It might be national, like a major holy day (Christmas), or local, like a patron saint's day (Saint Rosalie). Something like a coronation might be the occasion for a *cuccagna*. Italy now has several annual secular holidays.

A *sagra* was more typically tied to a local food or crop. In our list there's a lot of "crossover" between the two definitions. The feasts of Saint Joseph and Saint Lucy are associated with certain foods without being dedicated to them, while the artichoke and almond festivals are not religious except for prayers of thanks for a good harvest.

Almost every town has one or another annual sagra. Some have been held for centuries, others for just a few years. Our list is dedicated to the more traditional food festivals rather than those instituted over the last decade or celebrated only sporadically. It is not intended as anything like a complete list covering every Sicilian town.

It should be remembered that the dates for strictly culinary festivals vary somewhat from year to year. Therefore, this list should not be taken as authoritative. If you plan to attend any of these festivals, check the locality's website for scheduling during the *current* year before you plan your trip. (Many towns fail to update their websites very frequently, so be sure that you are reading about the *upcoming* festival, not the one held last year!) Here in Sicily, most towns finalize the date only two or three months before the event.

6 January: Epiphany, various Christmas specialties (see below). Ricotta Festival, Sant'Angelo Muxaro. Sfincia Festival, Montelepre.

20 January: San Sebastiano (St. Sebastian) ceremony and festival, Acireale.

1-15 February: Almond Blossom Festival (Sagra del Mandorlo in Fiore). Traditional folk festival in Valley of the Temples and city of Agrigento, with parades, shows, craft exhibits.

5 February: Feast of Saint Agatha (Sant'Agata), patroness of Catania. Processions, shows, exhibits, various foods.

March: Seppia (cuttlefish) Festival, Donnalucata Scicli.

Carnival Week (40 days before Easter): Carnival Celebrations (Mardi Gras or Shrove Tuesday), featuring parades of costumed actors and floats, games, holiday foods. Acireale, Sciacca, Termini Imerese. Classic dessert is *chiacchiere* (angel wings).

19 March: Saint Joseph's Day. Feast is celebrated around Sicily with sfinci di San Giuseppe, pasta with sardines, sfincione, breads, dinners. Major festivities at Salemi (votive bread), San Giuseppe Jato.

20-22 March: Tarocco (blood orange) Festival, Francofonte.

Late March: Artichoke Festivals at Niscemi and Ramacca.

Easter: Lamb and baby goat, artichokes, marzipan, cassata. Bread Festival at San Biagio Platani; features large, outdoor bread sculpture and arches, just before Easter.

April: Orange Festival, Ribera. Cannolo Festival, Piana degli Albanesi.

25 April: Ricotta Festival, Vizzini.

Late April: Artichoke Festival at Cerda; Fritella Festival at Isnello; Tomato Festival at Sampieri.

Early May: Strawberry Festival at Cassabile, near Siracusa, Cannolo Festival at Piana degli Albanesi.

Last Week of May: Turk's Head Festival, Scicli. The *Testa di Turco* is a sfincia shaped into the form of a turban.

Late May: Caper Blossom Festival, Salina (Aeolian Islands).

Early July: Peppered Mussel Festival, Aci Trezza.

14-15 July: Saint Rosalie Festival. Snails, semenza, torrone, watermelon.

Late July: Olive Oil Festival, Furnari.

Early August: Aubergine Festival at Milazzo; Cherry Tomato Festival at Pachino.

14-16 August: Onion Festival at Giarratana, Tortone Festival at Sperlinga (the *tortone* is a local cake), Wheat Harvest Festival at Gangi.

Late August: Sardine Festival in Selinunte; Seafood Festival in Mazara del Vallo; Peach Festival at Bivona.

15-18 September: Sherbet Festival dedicated to sorbets and ice creams at Cefalù; Sausage Festival at Aragona.

25-30 September: Couscous Festival. Culinary exposition featuring Sicilian and North African cuisine and events, San Vito Lo Capo.

October: *Ottobrata Zafferanese,* Zafferana Etnea, general festival held in the Etna region two or more weekends of the month featuring chestnuts, mushrooms, apples, honey.

6 October: Pistachio Festival, Bronte.

1-2 November: All Saints Day, All Souls Day. Marzipan, various desserts depending on locality. Sugar marionettes (now cartoon figures) or *pupi di zucchero,* and muffuletta bread with anchovies.

11 November: Saint Martin's Day; hard cookies and Muscat-based wine.

Late November: Wild Mushroom Festival, Caltavuturo.

Early December: Chocolate Festival, Modica.

6 December: Saint Nicholas; maccu (fava soup).

8 December: Immaculate Conception; sfincione, sweet fried sfinci.

12-13 December: Saint Lucy Festival in Ortygia district, Siracusa. Around Sicily, no flour products are prepared on this day. Cuccìa and arancini are popular.

25 December: Christmas; buccellato and cassata are popular.

CHAPTER 16

A Dozen Classic Recipes

"A good cook is like a sorceress who dispenses happiness."

— Elsa Schiaparelli

To make choosing and planning easier, our very concise collection begins with main courses, proceeds to pasta recipes, then side dishes and appetizers. We have made an attempt to "internationalize" measurements (quantity by weight is metric and American), and to include recipes containing ingredients most likely to be found outside Italy as well as here in Sicily, even if you may have to visit a gourmet grocer or an import store to find a few. Most of the distinctively Sicilian ingredients are described in the preceding pages or in the glossary. Yes, we know that the size of an aubergine is an imprecise measure; most of these recipes can be personalized to the chef's preference. There are fine cookbooks full of Sicilian recipes. Here we have sought to include a few traditional recipes which most cookbook authors overlook.

Chicken Marsala (Pollo al Marsala)

This dish was made famous with the growing Marsala wine industry early in the nineteenth century. Veal Marsala probably originated among western Sicily's English families.

Ingredients: Two large chicken breasts cut into thin slices (an equal quantity of turkey breast or lean veal may be substituted), one bottle of Marsala, whole or white flour, olive oil, 2 tablespoons of capers, juice of one large lemon, two tablespoons coarsely chopped fresh parsley, salt, pepper.

Preparation: Over medium heat, warm several tablespoons of olive oil in a large pan for a few seconds. Generously coat chicken pieces with flour and place in pan, turning it to cook both sides. Sprinkle with salt and pepper. Add juice of one lemon. When the chicken is essentially cooked, carefully pour a half bottle of Marsala wine over it, stirring the mixture gently. Allow alcohol to evaporate as sauce thickens. This may take about two minutes. Add the parsley when it's done. If you prefer a thicker sauce, add a little flour. Sprinkle capers last over the meat as a garnish. Serves four.

Red Mullet in Onion Sauce (Triglie di Scoglio)

In Sicilian waters, the best mullet and snapper are caught in the Spring. This dish, famous in Sicily's seaside communities, was a favorite of the aristocracy, with which it is strongly identified. The link is probably due to the rarity of good mullet during certain seasons. The use of cane sugar (introduced into

Sicily by the Arabs) and onions in this way is essentially a North African touch the Sicilians call *cipollata*. The sauce is also called *stemperata*.

Ingredients: Two red mullets about 16 centimeters (6 inches) in length, 2 large yellow onions sliced, whole grain or white flour, cup of white wine vinegar (a good varietal vinegar is best), five tablespoons of white sugar, two tablespoons of finely chopped fresh mint, olive oil, two eggs (well beaten), salt, mild white pepper.

Preparation: Clean the mullets but leave the heads attached. Liberally coat the fish with flour, dip them in the beaten eggs, and dredge them in flour again. Fry the mullets in refined olive oil over medium heat, turning at least once, until fully cooked. Remove mullets from pan and drain any excess oil by placing fish on absorbent paper. Discard frying oil. Very slowly sauté onions in virgin olive oil in a separate pan. When cooked, add about a half cup of vinegar. Add sugar and stir mixture. When sugar begins to thicken, add salt and pepper to taste. Remove pan from heat. Add mint. Add cooked mullets, or place the fish on a plate and pour the sauce over them. Serve with a large slice of lemon. Some traditionalists believe this dish is best served slightly chilled or at room temperature. Serves two.

Stuffed Squid (Calamari Ripieni)

This is one of the many simple yet delicious seafood dishes for which Sicilian cuisine is famous. The success of this recipe depends on the freshness of the ingredients, although we have used frozen squid and shrimp in a pinch. It's healthy, and easy to prepare.

Ingredients: Four large squid (any variety is acceptable but the body should be about 20 centimeters or 8 inches long), one pound (half kilogram) of bread crumbs, 8 chopped prawns (jumbo shrimp), 1 large chopped yellow onion, 3 eggs, 3 tablespoons of pine nuts, 3 tablespoons of raisins, 3 tablespoons of chopped capers, 2 tablespoons of chopped (fresh) parsley or mint, half tablespoon sweet paprika, salt and pepper, olive oil, half bottle of white wine.

Preparation: Preheat oven to 250 C (460 F). Clean squid; remove innards but leave the body whole. Mix (knead) all the filling ingredients (except the wine and olive oil) thoroughly into a paste. Add paprika, salt and pepper as desired, and as much water (at least a cup) as you need to maintain a suitable consistency. Stuff this into each cleaned squid. Using a fork with sharp tines, poke a few holes along the body of the stuffed squid. The tentacles may be tossed into the pan, in-between the squid. Take care not to "over stuff" each squid, as the filling will expand. Bake in a flat, oiled pan in the oven uncovered for 40-45 minutes. Check the squid every 8-10 minutes, sprinkling wine over them to avoid drying and to make a sauce (this will be violet or reddish depending on the squid variety). Serve with a lemon wedge. Salt to taste.

Caltanissettan Poultry Stuffing (Ripieno alla Nissena)

The residents of Caltanissetta, a small city in the Sicanian Mountains, are called *Nisseni,* and their mountainous region is famous for meat and poultry dishes. This simple recipe offers a pleasant alternative to meat-based chicken or turkey filling. Since the size of the bird varies, consider these measurements proportional.

Ingredients: 1 cup finely chopped white or yellow onions, 1 cup grated sharp cheese (caciocavallo or pecorino), 1 cup bread crumbs, one half cup chopped fresh parsley, 3 eggs, one-half teaspoon ground white pepper (black pepper may be substituted), salt to taste.

Preparation: Mix the ingredients in a large bowl, kneading the mixture until it's uniform in consistency. Add a little water if necessary to make it more workable. Then stuff the mixture into the cavity of the chicken or turkey before roasting. In Sicily, the chicken is sometimes garnished with fresh rosemary, and Marsala wine is poured over it at several points during the baking.

Trapani-style Pesto (Pesto alla Trapanese)

This Sicilian version of the classic Ligurian basil pesto emerged during the eighteenth century in Trapani and Erice. Is it connected to sailors from Genoa? We may never know, but there were Genoese communities in Palermo and other western Sicilian cities.

Ingredients: One cup of fresh basil leaves, 2 small cloves of peeled garlic (or 1 large clove), 1 tablespoon white (skinned) almonds, 1 tablespoon pine nuts, 5 tablespoons extra virgin olive oil, 3 large peeled (and steamed) tomatoes chopped into cubes, salt and pepper to taste.

Preparation: Slice the garlic cloves. Grate all the ingredients except the tomatoes in a blender for a few seconds with two small ice cubes until finely chopped but not pureed. (The ice keeps the temperature low and prevents the basil from darkening while enhancing liquidity.) Mix the tomatoes into the sauce. Add more olive oil if preferred, and mix into thick spaghetti or linguini. This serves four.

Pasta with Cauliflower (Pasta con Cavolfiore)

This is a seasonal dish served from October to April. Like the others, it has many local variations.

Ingredients: 2 cups cauliflower florets (preferably green broccoflower), thick spaghetti, extra virgin olive oil, 1 medium onion finely chopped, 1 teaspoon powdered saffron, 5 large anchovies, 2 tablespoons raisins, 2 tablespoons pine nuts, salt, pepper.

Preparation: Boil the cauliflower. In the meantime, in a large frying pan, sauté the chopped onion in the olive oil. Add the cauliflower and mix it with a wooden spoon until it becomes soft and breaks up into a loose paste. Add the saffron, anchovies, raisins and pine nuts. Add to hot pasta. (Ideally, the pasta should be boiled in the water used to cook the cauliflower.) Serves four.

Mollica: One may sprinkle cheese over this pasta, but a mixture of "toasted" bread crumbs, *mollica,* is traditional in Sicily. To make this, finely chop two large cloves of garlic. Brown these garlic pieces in olive oil over low heat. Then add a cup of bread crumbs. Stir constantly for just a few minutes until slightly browned. Remove from heat and immediately dump into a china or ceramic bowl (to prevent further toasting). Allow to cool. Serve at room temperature.

Fave with Artichokes (Fritella or Fritedda)

This green Spring dish is prepared with fava beans (green broad beans), artichokes and peas. It is essential that all the ingredients be absolutely fresh because that's what makes fritella tasty. The fava beans should be green fava (Vicia Faba Linnaeus). We suggest wild artichokes (the kind with thorned leaves) and fresh, unfiltered olive oil. Fava beans are a healthy food. However, people who suffer from the rare but potentially fatal condition called "favism" (hemolytic anemia or G6PD deficiency) should not consume fava beans, which may also affect individuals suffering from certain forms of thalassemia.

Ingredients: Equal parts of fresh fava beans, artichoke hearts (with tender leaves), fresh peas, six tablespoons raw, unfiltered extra virgin olive oil, salt.

Preparation: Chop up hearts and tender (edible) leaves of artichokes. Boil the fava beans until tender; discard water. Boil peas and artichokes, adding fava beans when the other ingredients are nearly cooked. Then let the mixture simmer for 3 or 4 minutes. Strain any excess water, sprinkle with olive oil and salt to taste. This recipe may also be used as a condiment (sauce) for pasta.

Potato Croquettes (Crocchè di Patate)

This is a favorite street food in Sicily, but for centuries it was something made at home.

Ingredients: half kilogram (1 pound) potatoes, 2 eggs, 2 tablespoons flour, 4 tablespoons grated caciovallo cheese, 3 tablespoons fresh mint (finely chopped), 3 tablespoons fresh parsley (finely chopped), salt and black pepper, vegetable oil (for frying).

Preparation: Boil the potatoes until soft enough for a fork to poke through them. Strain, and cool for a few minutes. Peel the potatoes and mash them in a large bowl. Set them aside to cool completely. Once they have cooled, add the eggs, flour, cheese, mint, parsley, salt and pepper, and mix well. With your hands, fashion the croquettes in an oblong form. Each one should be about 5 centimeters (2 inches) long.

In a heavy saucepan, heat a depth of at least 5 centimeters (2 inches) of vegetable oil over a medium flame until hot. Fry the croquettes in small batches until golden brown on all sides, about 2 minutes per batch, turning as needed. Drain on paper towels. Serve warm. This recipe serves eight.

Sfincione (Sicilian Pizza)

This is a popular street food but also made at home. Most regions of central and southern Italy have their own native forms of pizza or focaccia. This is Sicily's.

Dough Ingredients: 1 kilogram (2.2 pounds) flour, 50 grams (2 ounces) fresh compressed cake yeast (or 2 tablespoons of active dry yeast), 1 cup extra virgin olive oil, 1 tablespoon salt, 2 tablespoons sugar, 2 cups milk, 1 cup water, 1 mashed potato.

Preparation of Dough: In a very large bowl (the dough will double in size as it rises), mix together the flour with the potato, sugar and salt. Gradually add the water and olive oil and start mixing the ingredients with your hands, making a "hole" in the middle of the mixture. Dissolve the yeast in some lukewarm milk and pour it into the center of the flour mixture. Blend together with your hands. Continue kneading for about 15 minutes. The dough has to be very soft. Cover with a damp cloth and set in a warm place for one hour to let the dough rise.

Topping Ingredients: 1 kilogram (2.2 pounds) pureed tomatoes, 2 large peeled tomatoes chopped, 4 finely chopped yellow onions, 5 tablespoons chopped preserved anchovies, 1 cup extra virgin olive oil, 2 tablespoons sugar, 1 tablespoon oregano.

Preparation of Topping: Chop the onions thinly or else mince them finely in a mixer. Place them in a large frying pan with the olive oil. Cover and simmer until the onions start to wilt and become transparent. Remove the oil from the anchovies and add them to the onions. Cook at low heat until the anchovies dissolve into the onion mixture, but do not let the sauce brown. Add the pureed tomatoes and cook for 15-20 minutes. Once the sauce is cooked, remove from heat, stir in the tomato chunks, oregano and sugar. Let it cool completely.

Baking: Heat the oven to 220 degrees C (425 F). Use two rectangular baking sheets (around 41 x 28 cm or 16 x 11 inches) to make the sfincione pizzas. Grease the baking sheets with olive oil. Divide the dough into two equal parts and spread it out thinly onto the pans by using your hands, previously greased in plenty of olive oil, to flatten out the dough evenly onto the baking sheets. You should get a pizza dough that is about one centimeter, or half an inch, thick. Spread the sauce uniformly over the sfincione.

Place in hot oven and cook until the crust is golden underneath, but not burned, 30-40 minutes. (Optional: Sprinkle grated cheese over the sfincione 5 minutes before removing it from the oven.) Serves eight.

Aubergine Salad (Caponata)

It is said that the name for this salad derives not from *caper* but from *capone,* the dolphin fish, chunks of which were added to it in former times. Like most Sicilian recipes, this one has many slight variations. A popular version uses artichokes rather than aubergines. Ours is the simplest.

Ingredients: 4 unpeeled aubergines (eggplants) cut into 1.5 centimeter (half inch) cubes, half cup pureed tomatoes, 2 celery stalks cut into 1.5 centimeter (half inch) segments, 1 sliced yellow onion, half cup of capers, 1 cup pitted green olives, 2 tablespoons of pine nuts, 5 tablespoons white vinegar, extra virgin olive oil, salt, sugar.

Preparation: Cook the aubergines in a pan with olive oil, stirring frequently; remove and strain. With the remaining liquid and a few tablespoons of added oil, sauté the onions until cooked, adding a few spoons of water and two tablespoons of sugar. Then add the celery, which should be lightly cooked but not too soft or soggy. When this mixture is cooked, add the capers, tomatoes and olives, along with the aubergines and vinegar. Simmer this complete mixture for 5-7 minutes over medium heat. Caponata may be served slightly chilled or at room temperature, either as a salad or with toast.

Sicilian Orange Salad (Insalata d'Arance)

This classic recipe serves four.

Ingredients: 3 large navel oranges, 1 bulb anise, 4 tablespoons extra virgin olive oil, 2 boned smoked herring fillets (or sardines) cut into bite-size pieces, 1 tablespoon sugar, small pinch sea salt (less than a teaspoon), sugar.

Preparation: Cut off the top and bottom of the oranges and slice the fruit into segments about 1 centimeter (a half inch) thick. Place in a large bowl. Clean the anise and slice into segments of similar thickness. Add the smoked herring. Sprinkle on olive oil, orange juice and sugar. Salt according to taste. Serve at room temperature.

Zabaglione (Egg Nog)

This is the Sicilian version of the traditional winter drink usually made with rum or strong brandy. It goes well with cookies.

Ingredients: 2 liters (or quarts) of whole milk, one-half cup heavy cooking cream, 4 large egg yolks, 1 whole egg, 6 tablespoons refined white sugar, 14 tablespoons or one-half cup of sweet Marsala, nutmeg.

Preparation: Beat the sugar into the eggs, then add milk and cream for a smooth mixture, whisking constantly. Whisk the Marsala into the mixture, adding a pinch of nutmeg to taste. Continue to beat the mixture occasionally, increasing the volume slightly so that it is creamy. If you prefer, mix the ingredients in a blender at low speed for a few seconds. Serve chilled.

GLOSSARY

Most of these entries are simple translations from Italian or Sicilian, while some are necessarily more explanatory. A few are historical; we don't imagine that you'll be invited to a *cuccagna* in the near future. English terms such as *bar* are defined based on their Italian usage. Some additional terms are given, or elaborated upon, in the chapters. Note that Sicilian lacks a standard orthography, hence *monsù* and *monzù*. Mainstream Italian terms like *scaloppina* and *pinot bianco* are generally omitted.

agghiata - local word for *ghiotta* (a tomato sauce) in Messina. In Catania *agghiata* is a local recipe for *salmoriglio*.

agnello - lamb.

agrodolce - any sweet and sour sauce.

Altare di San Giuseppe - Saint Joseph's Banquet.

amaro - bitters.

ammogghiu - a thick, oily tomato sauce.

anelletti - pasta formed into small rings, used in Sicilian baked macaroni.

anice - anise.

anise fennel - anise greens, as opposed to wild "mountain" fennel. See *finocchio*.

anguilla - freshwater or sea eel.

anguria - red water melon, sometimes *melone rosso*.

antipasto - appetizer, starter.

aperitivo - aperitif.

arancina - fried rice ball filled with meat, irregular plural is *arancini*.

arborio - white rice native to Italy.

arrosto - roast.

babbaluci - small snails (in Italian, lumache).

baccalà - salted cod fillets in water.

baccalaru - Sicilian for baccalà.

badduzze - meat balls.

Ballarò - street market in Palermo at site of Fatimid souq.

bar - drink and coffee establishment, as distinguished from a pub.

beccafico - fresh roasted herring (sardines) stuffed with a mixture of traditional ingredients.

Biancolilla - Sicilian olive variety.

biancomangiare - almond blancmange.

birra bionda - light beer or ale, as distinguished from dark beer (stout or bock) or red beer.

biscotti del convento - "convent cookies," simple white flour biscuits made around Caltanissetta.

biscotto - cookie or biscuit (contrary to popular usage outside Italy, not a specific kind of cookie).

bistecca - steak.

bocconcini - any meat, bread or cheese formed into small pieces.

bollito - beef boiled in its own broth with vegetables and herbs.

bottarga - dried tuna roe.

broccoli - in Sicily this is sometimes the "green cauliflower" or broccoflower. See also *sparacelli.*

brodo - broth.

bruschetta - toasted bread topped with chilled chopped tomatoes, onions, olives and herbs.

bucatini - thick pasta similar to spaghetti with a hole running through the center.

buccellato - a crusty winter cake having a sweet filling of figs and nuts, sometimes cut into sections or formed into cookies.

cacio - old Sicilian word for cheese, cognate to *casein.* Sometimes *cascio.*

caciocavallo - a local cheese made from sheep's milk.

cacocciulo - Sicilian for *carciofo,* artichoke.

caffè macchiato - an *espresso* to which a small amount of milk has been added.

caffètteria - coffee shop, *bar* being the term usually used in Sicily.

calamari - squid.

calzone - bread roll baked with ham, cheese or other fillings.

canestrato - a cheese.

cannolo - pastry having a tubular crust filled with ricotta cream filling.

Capo - street market in Palermo near old Carini Gate.

caponata - cold salad of eggplant (aubergines), capers, olives, celery and tomatoes. A popular variation is made with artichokes instead of eggplant, and historically aubergine caponata contained chunks of capone (see below).

capone - dolphin fish.

capra - goat meat.

capretto - young goat; kid.

capricciosa - a pizza made with numerous ingredients, including tomatoes, mozzarella, ham, artichokes, olives and other toppings.

cappuccino - light coffee served with steamed milk and usually served at breakfast, named for its color resembling that of the light brown habits of Capuchin monks.

carciofi - artichokes.

carduna - cardoon, celery-like stalk of a plant related to the artichoke.

Carolea - Sicilian olive variety.

cassata - cake or tort of sweet ricotta cream filling in a crust of frosting and candied fruits.

Castiglione - Sicilian olive variety.

Cataratto - white grape of Sicily.

cedro - citron.

cefalo - the flathead mullet *mugil cephalus*.

cena - usually supper (evening meal) but sometimes a large lunch.

Cerasuola - Sicilian olive variety, also known as *Ogliara*.

cernia - Mediterranean grouper.

chiacchiere - crisp pastry made of flattened dough, sweetened with sugar; *angel wings* similar to French *bugnes* and German *raderkuchen*.

chitarre - literally guitars, spaghetti whose shape is square rather than round, formed by running the soft paste through a series of wires similar to the strings of a guitar.

cipollata - glaze of onions, vinegar and sugar used as sauce for certain fish dishes. Also *stemperata*.

cocuzza - a long green squash (actually a gourd), also *cucuzza*.

colazione - breakfast. Also *prima colazione*.

condimento - condiment; usually refers to the toppings on a pizza.

confetti - almonds coated with white or opaque-colored sugar.

coniglio - rabbit.

conto - restaurant check.

contorno - a side dish, usually in addition to the salad.

coperto - nominal cover charge added to restaurant bill, usually one or two euros per person; this is not a tip.

cornetto - light breakfast pastry similar to a croissant.

cotognata - quince preserves.

cotoletta - breaded beef, pork or poultry cutlet.

couscous - Tunisian pasta dish popular in western Sicily.

cozze - mussels.

crastuni - an edible snail, *helix aspersa maxima*.

cremeria - an ice cream shop, in Sicily *gelateria* is the more common term.

crispella - fritter stuffed with either ricotta and anchovies (salty version), or coated with honey (sweet version).

crocchè - Italian spelling of *croquette*. (See below.)

croquette - fried potato and cheese dumpling.

cubaita - sesame brittle.

cubaita di mandorla - almond brittle, sometimes *torrone di mandorla*.

cuccagna - abundance of food; historically, a festival offering a great variety of food to the poor of a large city.

cuccìa - traditional winter cream pudding made from hard wheat, similar to rice pudding. Served on Saint Lucy's Day, 13 December.

cucina povera - simple cookery based on traditional country recipes.

cucuzza - See cocuzza.

cus-cus - Italian spelling of couscous.

cuscusu - Sicilian for couscous.

Cynar - trade name for a bitter liqueur made from artichokes and various herbs.

denominazione di origine controllata - official appellations for wine, cheeses, olive oils (abbreviated DOC), similar to European *protected designation of origin.*

dolci - desserts.

espresso - simple Italian coffee, the presumed form of *caffè* unless specified otherwise; the word *espresso* may be used for any speedy service.

extra virgin - the highest grade of cold-pressed olive oil.

farina - flour. See also rimacinato.

farro - unmilled wheat grain.

farsumagru - or *falsomagro,* stuffed veal roll.

fatùk (or fastuca) - Sicilian for pistachio, from Arabic.

fava - a flat broad bean grown in Sicily.

fennel - See *finocchio.*

fichi d'india - prickly (cactus) pears.

filetto - fillet.

finnochio - fennel. The term actually refers to the wild variety, *finocchio di montagna,* not the anise greens often sold as *finocchio* nowadays.

focaccia - a seasoned bread, quite similar to a thick pizza, but flavored with olive oil and herbs instead of vegetables and cheese; the few focaccerias (focaccia bakeries) in Sicily serve focaccia but also sfincione.

frascatela - a doughy dumpling paste of cauliflower and bacon.

friggitoria - food stand specializing in fried foods such as panella, arancini, croquettes, etc.

frittata - an omelet, which in Italian cookery (as opposed to most French recipes) has the various ingredients mixed into the beaten eggs before cooking.

fritedda - vegetable dish or pasta sauce made with fresh green fava beans, peas, and artichoke hearts.

fritella - Italian for *fritedda.*

frittola - small pieces of fried beef offal. Also *fruttula.*

frizzante - describes effervescent water.

frutti di mare - seafood, such as shellfish and prawns (shrimp).

gamberi - shrimp.

gamberoni - large shrimp or prawns.

gattò - from the French *gateau,* potato, egg, cheese and meat filling in the form of a pie similar to shepherd's pie (cottage pie) or quiche.

gelateria - an ice cream shop.

gelato - ice cream, whether made with or without milk (there exists yogurt gelato).

gelo di mellone - sweet gelatine dessert made from water melon, served in Summer.

gelsi - mulberry.

gelsomina - jasmine, an ice cream flavored with this flower.

ghiotta - a fresh, simple tomato sauce made with olives and capers. Also *agghiata*.

Girgentana - breed of goat raised in the Agrigento (Girgenti) region, prized for its milk and wool.

giri - refers generically to any of several spinach-like chards.

Gorgonzola - Italian bleu cheese, named for the Lombard city where it is made.

granita - crushed sweetened ice flavored with lemon, strawberries, mint or mulberries.

grano duro - durum wheat used to make pasta.

grappa - strong brandy distilled from grape pumice and seeds.

griglia - grill; *alla griglia* refers to grilled dishes.

Grillo - white grape of Sicily.

insalata mista - salad of lettuce and other vegetables.

insalata riso - cold rice salad, a Summer dish.

Insolia, Inzolia - white grape of Sicily.

involtini - grilled or roasted chicken or beef slices stuffed with vegetable or meat filling; also aubergine slices and leafy vegetables (such as radicchio) stuffed with meat filling. *Involtini di spada* are swordfish rolls.

latte di mandorla - literally "almond milk," milky white drink made with sweetened almond paste and almond extract; sometimes mixed with carbonated water.

limoncello - generic name for a sweet lemon liqueur.

maccarone - pasta, especially in large pieces or thick strands. Also *macaroni*.

macchiato - See *caffè macchiato*.

maccu - also macco, creamy winter soup made from dried fava beans and fennel.

macinato - Sometimes *macinata*. See rimacinato.

maiorchino - cheese made in northeastern Sicily.

Malvasia - a dessert wine.

margherita - a pizza made with tomatoes, basil and mozzarella.

Marsala - fortified wine similar to Port, named for the Sicilian city where it is made; *al Marsala* refers to veal or poultry prepared with this wine.

martini - sweet white or red vermouth; unless the term "cocktail" is specified, this is not the cocktail of this name (containing dry vermouth with vodka or gin) but the vermouth itself.

martorana - in Palermo, marzipan shaped and colored to resemble fruit. Also *pasta reale.*

mattanza - method for capturing large tuna in a series of "chambers" formed by giant nets.

meuza - Sicilian for *milza.*

millefiori - honey made from blossoms of various wildflowers.

milza - sauteed veal spleen, usually served in sandwiches.

minestra - any simple vegetable soup or broth.

minni di vergini - See virgin's breast.

Modican chocolate - chocolate made in Modica using an old Aztec recipe.

mollica - dried bread crumbs, including those toasted with garlic sprinkled as a condiment over certain pasta dishes.

monsù - historical term for chefs in aristocratic homes, especially French cooks. Sometimes *monzù.*

Moresca - Sicilian olive variety.

Moscato - any Muscat-based wine; in Sicily such a wine made using a specific method.

muccuni - sea snails.

muffuletta - a round bread.

mustazzola - filled cookie made with almonds and honey.

naturale - natural; describes mineral water that is not effervescent; "still water."

Nebrodian swine - also *suino nero* (black pig), porcine species raised in the Nebrodi mountains.

neonata - baby sardines (a few days old) served as a sauce or fried.

Nero d'Avola - red grape of Sicily.

nero di seppia - cuttlefish (seppia) ink and the black sauce made from it.

nespoli - medlars or loquats; also Japanese loquats.

noce - walnut.

nocciola - hazelnut, an ice cream flavor.

Nocellara - Sicilian olive variety.

nucatoli - honey cookies.

'nzuddi - Catanian cookies made from almonds, oranges and cinnamon.

Ogliara - Sicilian olive variety, also known as *Cerasuola*.

osteria - literally a tavern or inn, but usually a *trattoria*.

ostriche - oysters.

palombo - smooth-hound (houndshark), a small, edible shark.

pan di Spagna - white sponge cake.

panella - flat fried cakes made with ceci bean flour, often served as an appetizer.

panino - sandwich.

Passito - a dessert wine made from a specific grape variety.

passolina - small, dark, sweet raisin.

pasta alla norma - Catanian pasta sauce made with aubergines (eggplants) and tomatoes.

pasta al forno - pasta baked with beef, tomatoes and cheese; similar to baked lasagne.

pasta con sarde - pasta dish made with herring, fennel and pine nuts.

pasta reale - almond paste marzipan decorated and colored to resemble fruits and various objects. See also *frutta martorana*.

pastella - batter, any food prepared in this way and fried

pasticceria - pastry shop.

pasticcio - pie or tart.

pecora, pecorino - describes ricotta and certain other cheeses made from sheep's milk.

Perricone - red grape of Sicily.

pesce - fish.

pesce spada - sword fish.

Pescheria - street market in Catania.

pesto - green pasta sauce made from ground, crushed basil and pine nuts; in Sicily there is also pistacchio pesto and Trapani-style pesto.

piacentinu - cheese of Enna region.

piccante - spicy.

pinoli - pine nuts.

pizzaiola - describes certain dishes, such as some sausages, and even potatoes, made with a variety of vegetable ingredients and spices.

pizzeria - restaurant specializing in pizza and certain fried foods.

pollo - chicken. *Pollo allo spiedo* is chicken on a skewer.

polpette - meatballs. See also *badduzze*.

polpo - octopus.

porcini - small dark mushrooms.

pranzo - lunch.

Primitivo - red grape of Sicily, Apulia and Balkans; Zinfandel.

primo - also *primo piatto,* first course, usually a pasta or rice dish.

primo sale - a sweet Sicilian cheese. See also *tuma.*

protected designation of origin - European standard for protection of appellations, abbreviated PDO

protected geographical indication - European standard for identification of products by region, abbreviated PGI.

provola - cheese from cow's milk, made in regional Sicilian varieties (Nebrodi, Ragusa, Madonie).

pub - British style pub or American style bar.

quaresimali - crunchy lenten cookies containing almonds, similar to Tuscan *cantuccini.*

quaruma - beef offal. Also *caldume.*

quattro formaggi - a pizza made with four cheeses, usually mozzarella, bleu (or gorgonzola), and local cheeses.

reginelle - small cookies coated with sesame seeds.

ricci - sea urchins, usually served raw.

ricotta - cottage cheese, which in Sicily is made from sheep's milk.

rimacinato - flour made from durum wheat. Sometimes *rimacinata* or *macinato*.

ripieno - stuffing or filling.

riso nero - rice sweetened with chocolate.

risotto - describes various *arborio* rice dishes.

ristorante - usually a more formal restuarant which serves evening meals and sometimes lunches, as opposed to a trattoria or pizzeria, which would be less formal.

rollò - roast made of beef stuffed with meats, cheeses and vegetables.

rosolio - originally a liqueur flavored with rose petals, now a generic term for similar products.

sagra - rural culinary festival with emphasis on local cuisine.

salmoia - salt water, especially when used to preserve olives.

salmoriglio - condiment served over grilled meats, poultry, fish, made from olive oil, lemon juice, parsley, sometimes mint.

salsa verde - any green pasta sauce similar to pesto.

salsiccia - pork sausage.

salsiccia pizzaiola - pork sausage stuffed with onions, tomatoes, mushrooms and other vegetables.

sarde - fresh small herring (sardines), usually served stuffed (beccafico) or with pasta and fennel (pasta con sarde).

sarde a beccafico - See *beccafico.*

scacciata - filled focaccia, typical of eastern Sicily. Also *scaccia.*

scaloppina - thin, tender slices of veal, sometimes chicken or turkey breast.

scampi - large shrimp or prawns.

scapace - method of cooking and then marinating vegetables; Frederick II is said to have enjoyed scapace to which fish and saffron were added.

scuma fritta - nested spaghetti fritters.

secondo - also *secondo piatto,* second course, usually the main meat dish of a meal.

semenza - mix of dried, toasted, salted seeds or nuts.

semifreddo - whipped dessert similar to mousse.

seppia - cuttlefish.

sfincia - also sfinci, fried puffed dough (cream puffs) filled with cream, especially the *sfingi di San Giuseppe* served on Saint Joseph's Day, 19 March, or coated with honey. Singular is sfincia. The common Neapolitan term is *zeppola.*

sfincione - a thick Sicilian pizza topped with tomatoes, onions and anchovies; rarely served in pizzerias but available in focaccerias, some bakeries, or from street vendors. (To Sicilians, sfincione is not considered *pizza,* which in Italy is by definition thin and crusty.)

siccia - Sicilian for seppia, cuttlefish.

sparacelli - a tasty broccoli variety similar to the undomesticated broccolo; in some localities, wild asparagus.

spatola - scabbard fish.

spiedini - meat and vegetables served on a skewer, similar to shish kebab.

spremuta - freshly-squeezed orange (or lemon) juice, as distinguished from *succo d'arancia,* the bottled variety.

spongato - ice cream served in a large cup.

spumoni - a tricolored, three-flavored (typically cherry, chocolate pistachio), Neapolitan ice cream virtually unknown in Italy today but still made in the United States, where it was introduced in the 1890s. (The American term *Neapolitan* for vanilla, chocolate and strawberry tricolored ice cream is based on its former identification with spumoni.)

stemperata - fish and seafood sauce made with onions, sugar and white wine vinegar, *cipollata.*

stigghiola - seasoned and grilled lamb or kid intestines served on a skewer.

'stratto - dense, unseasoned tomato paste; also *strattu* or *estratto.*

stuzzichini - simple appetizers, usually fried, such as miniature *arancini.*

tagliere - a cutting board, sometimes used in place of a platter to serve cheeses and hams.

tarocco - blood orange.

testa di Turco - form of *sfincia* made in and around Scicli.

timballo - baked pasta formed densely by a timbale (a small, deep pan).

tinniruma - or *tenerume*, green tips and leaves of Sicilian squash or Italian zucchini (the word is widely misused).

tonno - tuna or tunny; this is a tasty dark Mediterranean variety served fresh, nothing like the canned white tuna sold in supermarkets.

torrone - soft noughat candy made with honey, egg whites and nuts. (Not to be confused with Sicilian *torrone di mandorla*, below.)

torrone di mandorla - Sicilian term for *cubaita di mandorla* (almond brittle).

totani - a variety of squid.

trattoria - an informal restaurant.

triglie - also *triglie di scoglio*, red mullet.

tuma - a cheese.

tunisini - variety of eggplant (aubergine) having a light purple skin and a very white flesh.

vastedda - *tuma* or *primo sale* cheese when aged; also a certain type of bread roll.

Verdello - Sicilian olive variety.

vergine - literally *virgin,* describes a pure grade of olive oil made from the first cold pressing of the freshly harvested olives.

vino bianco - white wine.

vino rosso - red wine.

virgin's breast - *minni di virgini,* a filled pastry.

vitello - beef.

vitellino - veal.

vongole - clams.

Vucceria - street market in Palermo. Also *Vucciria.*

zabaglione - eggnog

zammù - an anise extract.

zeppole. See *sfinci.*

Zibibbo - a Muscat variety of grape cultivated in Sicily

zuccata - sugared squash preserves. Also *cucuzzata.*

zuppa - soup.

zuppa inglese - rum mix, an ice cream flavor.

EPILOGUE
Palermo 2015

Food speaks to us. It is a universal language that touches the soul. To your authors, it is part of a millennial Sicilian tradition, but also part of our familial heritage, a piece of personal history.

Readers wishing to complement this guide with a cookbook — something we wholeheartedly encourage — may find that a striking number of these are written by two kinds of gastronomes passionate about Sicilian food and wine.

First there are non-Sicilians discovering what Sicily has to offer. Most of their books are written in English, or in any case a language other than Italian, and they reflect something of an "outsider's view." A few of these writers are Italians from other regions of the country. Kudos to these Siculophiles.

Then there are books translated from the writings of islanders, "natives" who are rediscovering a cuisine with which they were already vaguely familiar, perhaps from childhood. We applaud their personal journeys.

Having spent much time abroad, your authors represent both worlds.

There is no single "authority" on Sicilian cuisine, no "definitive" guide. Our only *caveat* regarding cookbooks and food (and wine) articles is that the gentle reader take the more imaginative observations about our island's culture and culinary history with a few grains of salt.

Our focus here has been the "fusion" cookery of Sicily's long, eclectic history from antiquity until the middle of the nineteenth century. But history can be cyclic. Recent years have witnessed an influx of peoples in Sicily's cities. Arriving from countries across Asia and Africa, these new immigrants bring with them all manner of foods just as the Sicilians once introduced our island's cuisine in Britain, Canada and the United States.

In compiling the information in this book, there was no substitute for being in Sicily, and having roots here, where our mothers and grandmothers inherited recipes that had been preserved in our families for many generations. For as long as anybody can remember, fruits, vegetables and livestock were raised on our families' farms in places with melodious names like *Altarello*, once a royal hunting ground and the site of the Lombardo lemon groves, and *Polizello*, where the ancient Sicanians had an agricultural village long before the arrival of the Phoenicians, the Greeks or the Alios.

Bridging the gap between city and country, it is a magically delicious legacy, not only for us but for everybody who enjoys great food and wine.

We hope that you find your Sicilian culinary journey worth the effort, and we wish you pleasant travels.

Buon viaggio.

SOURCES

The documentary sources for the information contained in this volume are numerous and diverse, ranging from the fragmentary writings of Archestratus to the works of Apicius and Ovid to the books of folklorist Giuseppe Pitrè, and a few exceedingly rare "classic" cookbooks published in Italy before we were born. Pliny's *Natural History* was also useful.

Although a complete listing would be lengthy indeed, it is more than fitting that the reader be provided some general indications.

The historical archives of several convents and aristocratic families were consulted, and we also reviewed *riveli* (tax rolls) listing extensive agricultural information compiled from *circa* 1500 to 1815.

Historical tomes like Tommaso Fazello's *De Rebus Siculis,* published in the sixteenth century, were consulted, as well as works dedicated more specifically to viticulture or agriculture, such as Filippo Nicosia's *Il Podere Fruttifero e Dilettevole.* Also consulted was Antonino Venuti's landmark *De Agricultura Opusculum,* published in 1516 as the first "modern" treatise on Sicilian agriculture.

A few medieval sources, works like *De Arte Venandi cum Avibus,* a treatise authored by Frederick II, were perused in search of culinary information, yielding a few nuggets. The writings of Hugh Falcandus were consulted. Composed during the twelfth century, Idrisi's geography of Sicily also offers a few useful insights, while bin Jubayr's account of Sicily, though brief, is highly evocative.

For clues about the dietary practices of Sicily's medieval

Jews, a good source is *The Former Jews of this Kingdom* by Nadia Zeldes.

An invaluable guide to Sicilian agriculture and topography in the years immediately before 1860 is Vito Amico's *Dizionario Topografico della Sicilia*.

The authors of the epigraphs speak eloquently and sufficiently for themselves.

Historical frontispieces shown on the following pages:
Early printings of the *Natural History* of Pliny the Elder and the culinary guide of Apicius, first printings of *De Rebus Siculis* (1560) by Tommaso Fazello and *Il Podere Fruttifero e Dilettevole* (1735) by Filippo Nicosia.

C. PLINII
SECVNDI NATVRALIS
HISTORIAE LIBER
SECVNDVS.

An sit mundus, & an vnus. **CAP. I.**

VNDVM † & hoc, quod alio alio cœlum appellare libuit, cuius † *alias sit, & hoc, quodsu-* circunflexu teguntur cuncta, numen esse credi par est, æternum, im- *que talii ap-* mensum, neq; genitum, neq; interiturum vnquam. Huius extera inda- *pellaretibuit.* gare, nec interest hominum, nec capit humanæ coniectura mentis. Sa- cer est, æternus, immensus, totus in toto, imò verò ipse totum: finitus, & infinito similis: omnium rerum certus, & similis incerto: extrà, intrà, cuncta complexus in se, idemq; rerum naturæ opus, & rerũ ipsa natura. Furor est, mensuram eius animo quosdam agitasse, atq; prodere ausos: alios rursus occasione hinc sumpta, aut his data, innumerabiles tradi- disse mũdos, vt totidem rerũ naturas credi oporteret: aut, si vna omnes incubaret, totidem tamen Soles, totidemque Lunas, & cætera etiam in vno & immensa, & innumerabilia sidera: quasi non eadem quæstione semper in termino cogitatio- nis occursura, desiderio finis alicuius: aut, si hæc infinitas naturæ omnium artifici possit assignari, non illud idem in vno faciliùs sit intelligi, tanto præsertim opere. Furor est, profectò furor, egredi ex eo: & tanquam interna eius cuncta planè iam sint nota, ita scrutari extera: quasi verò mensuram vllius rei possit agere, qui sui nesciat: aut mens hominis videre, quæ mundus ipse non capiat.

De forma eius. **CAP. II.**

FOrmam eius in speciem orbis absoluti globatam esse, nomen in primis & consensus in eo mor- talium, orbem appellantium, sed & argumenta rerum docent: non solùm quia talis figura om- nibus sui partibus vergit in sese, ac sibi ipsa toleranda est, seque includit & continet, nullarũ egens *† quá subinde* compaginum, nec finem aut initium vllis sui partibus sentiens, nec quia ad motum, † quo subinde *verti.l mex ap-* verti debeat (vt mox apparebit) talis aptissima est: sed oculorum quoque probatione, quòd conue- *parebit.* xus mediusque quacunque cernatur, quum id accidere in alia non possit figura.

De motu eius. **CAP. III.**

HAnc ergo formam eius, æterno & irrequieto ambitu inenarrabili celeritate, vigintiquatuor horarum spatio circumagi, Solis exortus & occasus haud dubiè reliquère. An sit immensus, & ideò sensum aurium facilè excedens, tantæ molis rotatæ vertigine assidua sonitus, non equidem facilè dixerim, non herclè magis, quàm circumactorum simul tinnitus siderum, suosque voluen- tium orbes: an dulci quidem & incredibili suauitate concentus, nobis qui intus agimus, iuxta die- bus noctibusq; tacitus labitur mundus. Esse innumeras ei effigies animalium rerumq; cunctarum impressas, nec (vt in volucrum notamus ouis) læuitate continua lubricum corpus, quòd clarissimi A   authores

APICIUS,

SIVE,

LIBER DE RE COQUINARIA,

COMPOSITUS EX VARIIS TESTIMONIIS

SCRIPTORUM LATINORUM,

QUAE SELEGIT ET CONJUNXIT

GREGORIUS MAJANSIUS,

Generofus Valentinus, & Duodecemvir
Stlitibus judicandis in Regia Domo
& Urbe.

VALENTIAE EDETANORUM:

Apud FRANCISCUM BURGUETE,
ANNO MDCCLXVIII.

F. THOMAE FAZELLI.
SICVLI OR. PRAEDICA‑
TORVM.

DE REBVS SICVLIS DECADES DVAE, NVNC
PRIMVM IN LVCEM EDITAE.

HIS ACCESSIT TOTIVS OPERIS IN‑
DEX LOCVPLETISSIMVS.

CAVTVM EST PHILIPPI ANGLIAE, HISPANIAE,
Siciliaeq; Regis, Pauli. IIII. Pont. Max. ac Venetæ Reip. priuilegio, ne
cui has Decades de Siculis rebus ad decennium in eorum di‑
tione vel imprimere, vel alibi impreſſas venales
habere, neue in sermonē Italicū iniuſ‑
ſu authoris vertere ſub mul‑
Ha liceat.

I L

PODERE

FRUTTIFERO,

E DILETTEVOLE

DIVISO IN TRE PARTI,

Nelle quali s'infegna la coltura delle vigne, falceto, can-
neto, alberi fruttiferi, colla loro iftoria, e natura,
sì per vaghezza, come per bofco, orti, femi-
nati di frumento, orzo, legumi, col go-
verno de' Bovi, Vacche, Pecore, ed
ogn'altro, che può far vaga, e
fruttuofa una poffeffione.

D I

D. FILIPPO NICOSIA

BARONE DI S. GIAIME, E DEL POZZO,
Della Città di Nicofia

IN PALERMO MDCCXXXV.

Appreffo Angelo Felicella.

CON LICENZA DE' SUPERIORI.

ACKNOWLEDGMENTS

Thanks are due a great many people, some of whom are no longer among us.

Drawn largely from work we had written over the course of fifteen years, since around 1999, the manuscript required a fair amount of editing. We wish to express our gratitude to our publisher's editorial staff, working between New York and Palermo, for their work on the text and for the maps, photographs, illustrations and cover design.

There's a certain insight that comes with actually producing the foods we eat. For information on olive oil purity standards, and an oil producer's view of these, thanks to Antonella Titone, whose olive farm near Trapani produces what most experts (and numerous award juries) consider Sicily's finest organic olive oil. Thanks also to Count Filippo Testa, a dedicated vintner.

Thanks to the cooperative staff of the Palermo Archive of State, where we consulted documents spanning the last five centuries.

Posthumous thanks to our friend and colleague, the late Roberta Gangi, and the generous staff of the website *Best of Sicily,* where our articles, ranging from food profiles to restaurant reviews, have been read by millions over the last decade.

This book is dedicated to the memory of two women from whom we learned much. Anna Vitale was Francesca's mother. Grazia Alio was Jackie's aunt.

We thank our many readers for their kind suggestions and encouragement.

INDEX

This is intended as a ready reference, with most words in English. Additional terms are included among the entries in the Glossary. More specialized terms, such as wine, olive and cheese varieties, will be found in chapters dedicated to those topics.